Hole
in fun

Hole in fun

A Round of 18 Humorous Golf Stories

With some additional comments on Dufferdom from the Club-house

Edited by Peter Haining

Illustrated by Stan McMurtry
MAC of the *Daily Mail*

GUILD PUBLISHING
LONDON

This book is for my Father,

BILL HAINING

'Golf is nothing more than three acres and a ball, spleen on the green, a tee fight with clubs, a three-mile walk punctuated with perplexing problems of proper procedure, billiards gone to grass, marbles played with clubs, the sublime stooping to the ridiculous, a game in which the ball lies well and the player badly, and faith, hope, and charity gone to the dogs.'

THOMAS JAY

Believe Me

CONTENTS

FOREWORD

Funny things have been happening in golf for hundreds of years. Here are two good examples.

In September 1985, two golfers named Dean Sadler and his friend Dean Smith were about to play off the first tee at their local golf course. Dean Smith was looking rather nervous as he prepared to swing with a number 8 iron, and so Dean Sadler interrupted him. He had complete confidence in his friend's ability, Dean (Sadler) said, and to prove it he took off his shoe and sock, stuck his companion's tee between his toes, and placed the ball on top.

'Now hit it!' commanded the same Dean.

So Dean Smith did – and hit his friend's toe and broke it! A howl in one, a newspaper report later called the tragedy.

Almost four hundred years earlier, a couple of Scottish pals found the round they were trying to play on a course near Edinburgh ended equally dramatically. For according to the records still on view in that venerable city, in the year 1593, John Henrie and Pat Rogie were unceremoniously bundled off to jail and imprisoned 'for playing of the Gowff on the links of Leith every Sabbath the time of the sermonses.'

If you would like a further instance to underline my point, let me tell you that in America they run a competition each year at Sawgass in Florida to find the most awful golfer in the world. Those attempting to win can't be merely mediocre but have to be really *bad* to earn the title 'Worst Avid Golfer'. They also have to have played 21 rounds in a year.

According to the press, 1985 brought some truly outstanding contestants. There was Ray Walker who put 327 consecutive balls into the water at one infamous hole. Another golfer, Neil Hamlin, took 55 shots to complete one hole, while Michael Bush couldn't even hit his ball as far as the ladies' tee on 14 out of 18 holes. Also strongly fancied for the title was Richard Gonzales who struck his golf ball no fewer than 11 times to progress four yards. Another unnamed entrant was even said to have recorded a drive of *minus* nine yards!

Is it any wonder, then, when pondering on such achievements that Winston Churchill – a man of strong opinions but not much love of golf – once commented, 'Golf is a game whose aim is to hit a very small ball into an even smaller hole with weapons singularly ill-designed for the purpose.' Another famous personage – the writer, Mark Twain – was even more disparaging. 'Golf,' he said, 'is a good walk spoiled.'

There is no doubt that most people, however much they play golf, develop a love–hate relationship with the game. For at one moment it can transport a player to the realms of ecstasy, and at the next reduce him (or her) to impotent rage. Sometimes only the ability to smile or, better still, laugh, can save the day.

To the uninitiated it undoubtedly seems an extraordinary game played with even more extraordinary equipment in pursuit of a most improbable objective. Indeed, whenever I think of the point of golf, I am reminded of some lines from an old poem, *Golfiana*, by the Scotsman, George Fullerton Carnegie, written in 1833:

> 'O hole! tho' small, and scarcely to be seen,
> Till we are close upon thee, on the green;
> And tho' when seen, save Golfers, few can prize,
> The value, the delight, that in thee lies;
> Yet, without thee, our tools were useless all –
> The club, the spoon, the putter and the ball:

For all is done – each ball arranged on tee,
Each stroke directed – but to enter thee!'

Another more recent bard – unfortunately anonymous as far as I can discover – put it rather more humorously when he declared:

'Golf's a very funny game;
I never get it right.
You buy a ball for half a crown,
Then knock it out of sight.
You hunt around in weeds and thorns
And find it in its den,
And take a club and try to knock
It out of sight again!'

Although there has, of course, been a great deal of argument about the origins of the game (and doubtless there will continue to be for years to come) there are still certain truisms about golf. One old cynic I know who has played golf all his life without ever getting his handicap into the magical realm of the single figure, once told me the sport was rather like marriage. 'It looks easy to them as haven't tried it,' he enlightened me.

I imagine, though, that there will be a few readers of this book who haven't 'tried it' at some point – and knowing that, I'm sure they'll appreciate that while top class golf demands serious concentration and the fullest application of mind and muscle, it can still have its funny moments. Certainly, this fact has made itself very apparent to the illustrious group of contributors whose stories you are about to read. Golfers all, though of varying degrees of skill, and fine writers too, they have enjoyed the highs and lows, the drama and the hilarity that can be part of any eighteen holes, and from their own experiences – or those of others – created the gallimaufry of golf which follows.

'Funny game, golf, isn't it?' I once heard a naturally cheerful fellow comment in the clubhouse after a disastrous round in which he had got soaked by rain, broken one of his clubs and been beaten ten and eight. I nodded in agreement and offered him a drink to try and raise his dampened spirits.

At that moment, his opponent came into the bar and, over-hearing the remark, replied without a trace of emotion:

'Yes,' he said, 'but it was never meant to be.'

Perhaps of all the examples of golfing humour I have heard, one stands above all the rest as somehow neatly encompassing all the mystique of the game.

'Do you play golf?' one man is said to have asked another.

'No,' came the reply, 'but I can't give it up!'

PETER HAINING
Boxford, Suffolk.
January, 1988.

1

A TALE OF GOLF

by *William Graham*

According to my Scottish ancestors there is no doubt that it was *our* kinsmen who invented the game of golf – despite the claims from Holland and elsewhere. Certainly there is evidence of it being played north of the border as far back as the middle of the fifteenth century (when King James II tried to ban it because it was interfering with the archery practice necessary to safeguard the nation!), but equally I have heard it muttered that no Scotsman could have invented a game where it was possible to lose the ball! Such arguments – serious and light-hearted – aside, it is surprising to discover that golf was not the subject of a notable book until the year 1875. In that year, Robert Clark, a successful Edinburgh printer by trade but a golf enthusiast by inclination, published *Golf, A Royal and Ancient Game*, which he had compiled and printed himself.

Clark's enthusiasm for the game inspired him to scour golf club archives and records, as well as newspapers and magazines, in search of instructional articles, descriptive reports of courses, diary extracts, poetry and fictional tales. Although Clark modestly referred to his anthology as 'but a collection of Scraps and Patches', he effectively brought together everything of real worth that had been written about the game. And as one might expect of a man in his line of business, the volume was beautifully illustrated and printed. Today, copies are of the utmost rarity, though a commercially-produced second edition issued in 1893 is a little easier to come across, but by no means cheap to purchase!

Several of the poems in the book have some light-hearted reflections to make about golf (one, for example, consists of

nine sonnets on the then nine holes at St. Andrews!) but there
is only a single piece of fictional prose by a humourist, written
by one William Graham, a professor at Edinburgh University
and a keen member at St. Andrews. Graham was apparently a
man who played golf with a cool determination matched to a
dry wit which made him an excellent partner but a tricky
opponent. He wrote 'A Tale of Golf' in 1873, and although it is
now well over a hundred years old, there is still a freshness
about its telling that makes it a delight to read – as well as
providing an ideal opening to our round. . .

A TALE OF GOLF

On the morning of the 17th August 183–, two native golfers of the famous Dubbieside, in Fife, were seen resting on the brow of the links and anxiously casting their eyes in the direction of Methill, as if expecting the smoking funnel of the ever-restless 'St. George'. Their coats of business were donned, their caps were drawn resolutely over their brows, and they examined with more than common care the knitting of their clubs, the insertion of the lead, and the indentation of the bone. From their capacious pockets they turned out ball after ball with mysterious care,[1] and the names of the makers were inter-changed with reverential whispers, as they peered into one or

[1] The balls were then made of leather, stuffed so full of feathers as to be at once hard and elastic.

two of the most select. At their feet reclined their caddies, grasping each a complete establishment of clubs, and listening with deep respect to the conversation of their masters. At last a towering column of smoke announced that the steamer was at hand, while from the end of the bank the florry[2] boat was plying its way to receive the passengers for Leven. The sportsmen leaped to their feet as the passengers descended the side of the steamer, and an exclamation of 'He's come!' burst from them as they saw a large package of clubs lowered down into the boat. They hastened to the sands to welcome the arrival of the stranger sportsman, who had been sent to dim the glory of Dubbieside; and there in the stern of the boat, with his arm encircling his instruments of play, did they behold the doughty champion, who was backed against the rustic players by some discomfited metropolitans, and who was destined to open the eyes of Dubbieside to its ignorance and vanity in assuming an equality with the clubs south of the Forth.

He was a short, stout-made, sandy-whiskered man; his spectacles not altogether concealing his ferrety eyes; his nose short, and ever ready to curl; and his lip compressing itself, as if it were bridling up under some slight or insult. He was the ideal of small pomposity, set off with a finical attention to dress; rings clasped his little fat fingers, and a diamond pin shone in his puffy breast. He surveyed his new brothers on the shore with an air of loftiness, although he must have known them for his intended associates and opponents, and cast on the country round a vexed look, as if his friends had compromised his dignity by sending him to a place that appeared so questionable. His stateliness, however, gave way to rage and abuse, when he found that to get ashore he must mount on the back of one of the boatmen. This mode of landing is seldom resorted to now – to ladies it was a torturing thought to be obliged to submit to be carried like babies through the breakers by some staggering boatmen who resented their fidgety movements by muttered threats of committing them to

---

[2] The boat which conveyed passengers ashore from the steamer at places where there was no pier, or when the tide would not allow the landing at the pier.

the deep, or of pinching them unceremoniously. No less torture was felt by our indignant golfer, but there was no alternative. He was horsed amid the smiles of passengers and
onlookers – his legs drawn up most ungracefully to save his
boots from the brine, and his face, over the shoulder of his
carrier, suggesting the appearance of the man of the moon in a
state of excitement. Arrived at the shore, he was set down with
little ceremony, when unluckily, his first contact with the
county of Fife was a sudden seat on the cold wet sand. He was
soon put on his legs by his brother sportsmen, whose mixed
condolence and banter were ill-calculated to soothe his
ruffled feelings; but with a tremendous effort the high pressure
gentleman readjusted his spectacles, and did assume enough
of calmness to look contempt on all around, and discharge an
execration at the county of Fife and the disgraceful incommo-
diousness of its conveyances.

The party now moved to the hole from which they were to
strike off, the stranger receiving the proposal of a short pause
at the public-house of the village with a look of horror. They
were here joined by a number of second-rate golf men, and old
lovers of the game who could yet, in despite of rheumatism,
follow the rounds – besides a whole troop of ordinary vil-
lagers, inspired, if not with a love of golf, at least with an
interest in the honour of Dubbieside. The stranger having
undone his clubs, round which his red coat was tightly roped
– having renounced his handsome green one with gilt anchor
buttons, and relinquished it with a sigh, and a shrink of
composure to his fate, to a Dubbieside caddie, whom he
looked on as a second Caliban, addressed himself to the
business of the day. He cast on the ground a 'Gourlay', white
as snow, hard as lead, and elastic as whalebone; and the
trembling caddie having, amid the whizz of a shower of novel
oaths, teed it at last to his satisfaction, he seized a club which,
like Cuttie Sark in Tam o'Shanter, was a 'supple jaud and
strong', and gave it a few preparatory vibrations – then assuming the honour of precedence, he addressed his body to his
ball, raised his club, and came round with a determined
sweep. The missile sped right into a sandy brae, which the
generality of players clear with the first stroke; but such a

thing will occasionally happen with the best player. So little was thought of it, though the testy stranger glowed like a red herring; and his humour was by no means restored when he saw his partners, after 'licking their looves', make their balls fly like sky-rockets over the place where he was earthed. Away, however, the crowd moved – principals, caddies, amateurs, club-makers, weavers, and hecklers – the last class of gentlemen having at this time struck for an advance of wages, and being glad of anything about which to occupy themselves. The whole formed a ring round the stranger gentleman, who was now to dig his ball out of its lodgement of sand. The occasion, the company, the awkwardness of his position, and the consciousness of the want of sympathy in all around, contributed to heighten the angry feelings of the champion; so, darting a glance of fire at one of the hecklers, who remarked with tipsy gravity, and most offensive familiarity, in allusion to the hopeless situation of the ball, that it would require spectacles to find it out, he gave it such an ill-natured and ill-directed whack, that it sank completely into the regions of night. The hurrays of the hecklers, the yells of the boys, the placid laughter of the paralytic old players, who shook upon their sticks, and the condolence of the rival players, which was given in all the offensiveness of Scotch diminutives, now nearly threw the mortified stranger into a fit of apoplexy. The ball, however, was declared not playable; and being dug out by the fingers of the caddie was thrown back on the green, at the loss of a stroke in counting to its owner. So, reconcentrating his energy, and assuming as much calmness as could be collected in a composition so formed, he aimed a well-directed stroke. Unfortunately, at the very instant, a prophetic groan or hem from one of the flax-tearing fraternity gave a wrong turn to the blow, and swept the ill-destined ball into a bunker or sand hole. Another cheer for Dubbieside was about to be raised, when the enraged stranger grappled with the obnoxious heckler, and lustily called for a constable. This produced a rush from his companions, who in an instant released him from the clutch of the indignant golfer, around whom the released heckler began dancing and sparring, with his jacket and paper cap doffed, demanding a ring and fair play. But the honour of the links being at stake, the Dubbie-side players laid hands on the shoulders of the rioters, and awed them into civility; so, after a few grumblings, the Dubbieside men having taken their second strokes which sent their balls far into safe and beautiful ground, the troop once more moved on. The metropolitan champion was now to strike his fifth stroke, or three more, and the perspiration stood in beads on his brow when he came up and beheld his infatuated Gourlay sitting as if in an egg-cup of sand. The more civilised of the idlers felt something like sympathy, and a feeling of commiseration was beginning to steal over the multitude, and when the caddie, having given the *cleek* instead of the *iron*, which the gentleman swore was the proper instrument, the said caddie was unceremoniously deposed with a cuff in the neck that sent him sprawling in the sand, and the clubs were at the same time wrenched from him by his irate master, who swore he would carry them himself. This event did not make the player more cool, or the spectators more indulgent; so when the ball was jerked from its position, it went slant over the bank to the firm bed of sand on the beach, when it rolled as on an iron floor till it cooled itself in the sea. The flaxmen, swinging arm-in-arm to the top of the bank, now burst out with a chorus of –

> The sea – the sea – the open sea,
> I am where I would ever be, etc.

This was too much. For a moment a sort of stupor seemed to fall on the devoted stranger; but an unearthly calmness and paleness succeeded, as he moved leisurely to the sea, picked up his ball, and put it into his pocket. He had observed the steamer on its return from Largo, and walking leisurely to the florry boat which was just going out, he arrived in time to secure his passage. His exit might have been dignified – for even the hecklers remarked that there was something 'no cannie in his look' when he left the ground, and they did not even venture to cheer – but just as the boat was shoving off, a frenzied-looking woman, running along the beach, made signs for the boat to stop, and in an instant the mother of the dismissed caddie was in the boat demanding his pay, and reparation for the damage done to her bit laddie. The approach of the obnoxious hecklers to witness this new scene, operated more on the discomfited golfer than the woman's clamour – and a bonus, most disproportionate to the damage, was slipped into the horny fist of the outraged mother, who, suddenly lowering her tone, stood upon the beach his only friend. Yet could she not, as the boat moved off, prevent the flaxmen sending after him their chorus of 'The sea, the sea', until he was seen to ascend the steamboat and suddenly disappear below.

Who or what he was remains a mystery; his backers never gave his name, or a hint of his profession. Some imagined him to be a principal Edinburgh clerk; others, a half-pay resident in Musselburgh; but who or what he really was, could not be discovered by the most curious inquirer.

2

THE CHELAH'S ROUND

by Andrew Lang

Aɴᴏᴛʜᴇʀ contributor to Robert Clark's anthology was Andrew Lang, a writer-enthusiast who in time was to become known as the 'Poet Laureate of Golf'. Lang primarily wrote about the game in verse, and the various poems to be found in his *Collected Works* range from the almost lyrical to the quite farcical. Few other poets have better captured the diverse nature of golf and its players in their work.

Andrew Lang was born in Selkirk, but it was while he was studying at St. Andrews University that he took up golf and also began writing about the sport. In time, he was to move south to London where he became a prolific journalist and author – writing on many aspects of mythology and folk tales – but he never neglected the chance of a game of golf with some of his literary friends. It was the golfing poems that he began to write from the 1870's onwards that earned him the title of the game's first 'Laureate' – an honour bestowed upon him by Horace Hutchinson, the famous amateur golfer and commentator on the sport, who also wrote one of the earliest novels about the game, *Bert Edwards, The Golf Caddie*, at the turn of the century.

Aside from the poetry, Lang produced a number of essays on the playing of the game, as well as several short stories and a sequence of 'historical' tales about supposedly famous golfers from the past including 'Socrates on the Links', 'Herodotus in St. Andrews' and 'Dr Johnson on the Links'. Funnier still than these – in my estimation – is 'The Chelah's Round', a story of an Indian mystic and some chicanery on the links. It has a finale which is amusing enough to leave the reader smiling long after he has finished. . .

THE CHELAH'S ROUND

I

The odds against John M'Gummidge's winning the Golf
Medal were, according to the Professor of Mathematics,
'humanly speaking, incalculable'. M'Gummidge was a
Freshman: he was long, lathy, ungainly, and wore spectacles. Never had he been seen on the Links, not even taking
solitary exercise with a short spoon. His only companion, a
singular figure, was a student from Northern Hindustan. The
Bobhachy Lal Rumun deserves a more particular description.
The snows of an unknown number of winters flowed over the
collar of his gown, while his silver beard (which in rainy
weather he tucked into his boots) gave him an aspect particularly venerable, but in no way sporting. Rumour ascribed to
the Bobhachy a longevity beyond the aspirations of romance,
and it was believed that ever since the days of Akbar he had
inhabited a cave in the Northern Himalayan slopes. A clear,

airy, tinkling sound, as of a claret glass lightly touched, which was occasionally heard when the Bobhachy was present – especially in Lecture – had in no way endeared him to his teachers. But as he explained that the mystic note was entirely beyond his own control, and merely meant that a Mahatma (or initiated Sage) in Tibet or Afghanistan was anxious to converse with him in the spirit, of course, censure was unjust and expostulation fruitless.

The Bobhachy could not be blamed, though it was remembered that the German Chelah in Mr Anstey's *Fallen idol* said – 'They are not gentlemen in Tibet'. Why the Bobhachy at his time of life (or trance rather) had sought a Northern University was variously explained. The most popular theory was that his parents had been too destitute to afford the usual fee for manners in Tibetan Colleges (two annas), and that he was now endeavouring, though late in life, to supply the deficiency of his early education.

The Bobhachy's mode of existence, like that of his only intimate (M'Gummidge), was solitary and far from gay. A cave under the Castle Rock, and just above high water, was thought to be their inexpensive lodging, and it was reported that they tasted nothing which had ever breathed the breath of life. A handful of pulse, the rain-water from the rock, served to nourish the fire of existence, which, on such fuel, burns 'with a hard gem-like flame', the Bobhachy said.

Though M'Gummidge was an assiduous attendant of philosophical lectures, there were some who whispered that under the teaching of the Bobhachy he was really pursuing that mystic or Esoteric Vedanta which has been successfully concealed from European inquisitiveness. In short, he was, perhaps, a 'Chelah', or pupil of the venerable old Hindu. News of this course of study could not but agitate the parental mind when it was conveyed to the distant shores of St. Kilda, and to the lonely manse where Mr M'Gummidge the elder tended his little flock. But still more surprise was felt, in golfing circles, when it was known that M'Gummidge had entered for the Medal. Layers never tired of offering odds fabulously long, which were snapped up by the Bobhachy. He was prepared, he said, to pledge even his *Cummerbund* (almost his only article of dress) rather than not be 'on' M'Gummidge to the extent of his available capital.

Whether the confidence of the patriarchal sage was justified is a question of which curiosity must be content to await the answer.

II

The great day of the Medal arrived. The Bobhachy himself carried for M'Gummidge. It was observed that his clubs were by no means new. But few spectators watched the start, M'Gummidge's companion being but an ordinary player, one Jones. The Bobhachy compiled however a business-like tee, and it was noted that M'Gummidge, as he addressed himself to his ball, displayed none of the diffidence of the novice. He lay near the burn, and a sough of the performance reaching the town, the odds fell from 10,000 to 1 to 10 to 1 against the Chelah. His second lay dead, and he holed out in three.

Then occurred a circumstance which none who saw it will ever forget. As his partner holed out in five, the strange mysterious tinkling note sounded on the green, and all eyes were fixed on the Bobhachy. The caddie who carried for Jones (M'Gummidge's companion) put his hand in the hole to take out the balls, and, as I am a living and honourable man, he exclaimed –

'O Heaven! what is this?'

Though two men had holed out, *there was but one ball in the hole.* As several credible witnesses had seen M'Gummidge's ball enter the hole, though none but Jones's came out, the Chelah was rated at three. The Bobhachy being pressed for an explanation observed that the Mahatmas in Tibet disapproved of 'Eclipses', and had probably disintegrated the mysterious matter of which 'Eclipses' are composed. He then put down a gutta, and M'Gummidge having the honour, struck off. His ball, being slightly 'toed', hit the old station-house, and cannoned back on to the green, where, after considerable search, it was found – in the hole!

'Great is Indra!' was the only remark of the Bobhachy. 'His throne doubtless has been unpleasantly warm.'

The devout Brahmin does indeed believe that the effect of prayer is to heat the throne of Indra, and to make him bestir himself in the cause of the Faithful. However this may be, the immediate effect was found in efforts to hedge among the layers of odds. Preying upon each other, in their terror-stricken cupidity, they brought the market round to 100 to 1 on the Chelah. When news came that he had gone out in thirty-seven (for he came to grief in the Eden, at the high hole, landing badly from the tee on the duck punt moored in the Estuary, where he could not lift his ball, and a 'mashie' had to be used) – when news came to this effect, the Links were crowded. The University, the Artillery, the Town, the Fishing population, the Clergy of all denominations, deserted their usual haunts and pursuits: three political meetings hastily broke up, the Cabinet Ministers and distinguished Fenians who had been addressing them were 'left speaking', and the whole agitated populace crowded round the Bobhachy, who by this time was talking in a remarkable Dundee accent.

Why pursue the narrative in detail? The Chelah's play may have been exaggerated by tradition, ever greedy for the mar-vellous. The stone bridge is reported to have broken down under the tread of the excited spectators, now swollen by the agricultural multitude. The records of the game, however, demonstrate that M'Gummidge did the round in 71, thereby breaking the record.

Next morning the town was full of newspaper reporters. But the Chelah and the Bobhachy were seen no more. Various theories as to the event have been promulgated. According to some, M'Gummidge was merely hypnotised by his dusky companion and caddie. If you can hypnotise an idle boy, so that he is head of his class while the influence lasts, as any one may read in the papers of the Psychical Society, why should you not do as much for a golfer? Others maintain that the whole affair was glamour. The Indian conjurer who does the mango trick, and makes a tree grow up before your very eyes from the seed in twenty minutes, must, it is argued, produce a 'collective hallucination' in the mind of the observer. (See *Psychical Society's Proceedings*.)

Others there were who declared that money was uncommonly plentiful on the Links of Leven and Carnoustie after the events which tradition has handed down. They averred that a long white beard, from Nathan's, and a 'Chestnut Bell', with a melodious tinkle, were found in a room of the Marine Hotel after the departure of two strangers who never paid their lawful debts to that establishment. And they insist that M'Gummidge was a novice from some obscure provincial 'green', while the Bobhachy was a speculative Club-maker and veteran professional in disguise.

So prone is the unaided human intellect to fly after mere natural explanations of events manifestly extra-natural.

3

THE DEVIL'S ROUND

by Charles Deulin

ANDREW LANG shared with Robert Clark a love of the printed ephemera of golf, and in 1892 published a collection of his own entitled *A Batch of Golfing Papers*. This he followed two years later with a history of St. Andrews which was replete with tales about the famous golf course.

Lang was particularly interested in the origins of golf and wrote at some length about the claims and counter-claims from Scotland, Holland and even France to have been the first to have played the game. During the course of his research he came upon the following amusing, not to say intriguing, tale by the Frenchman, Charles Deulin, about a canny golfer and his battle of wits with Old Nick. Lang included it in his anthology with the notes overleaf by way of introduction.

THE DEVIL'S ROUND

The following story, translated by Mrs Anstruther Thomson from *Le Grand Choleur*, of M Charles Deulin (*Contes du Roi Gambrinus*), gives a great deal of information about French and Flemish golf. As any reader will see, this ancient game represents a stage of evolution between golf and hockey. The object is to strike a ball, in as few strokes as possible, to a given point; but, after every three strokes, the opponent is allowed to *décholer*, or make one stroke back, or into a hazard. Here the element of hockey comes in. Get rid of this element, let each man hit his own ball, and, in place of striking to a point – say, the cemetery gate – let men 'putt' into holes, and the Flemish game becomes golf. It is of great antiquity. Ducange, in his *Lexicon of Low Latin*, gives *Choulla*, French *choule* = 'Globulus ligneus qui clava propellitur' – a wooden ball struck with a club. The head of the club was of iron (cf. *crossare*). This is borne out by a miniature in a missal of 1504, which represents peasants playing *choule* with clubs very like niblicks. Ducange quotes various MS. references of 1353, 1357, and other dates older by a century than our earliest Scotch references to golf. At present the game is played in Belgium with a strangely-shaped lofting-iron and a ball of beechwood. M Emile Zola, in *Germinal*, represents his miners playing *chole*, or *choulle*, and says that they hit drives of more than 500 yards. Experiments made at Wimbledon with a Belgian club sent over by M Charles Michel suggest that M Zola has over-estimated the distance. But M Zola and M Deulin agree in making the players *run* after the ball. M Henri Gaidoz adds that a similar game, called *soule*, is played in various departments of France. He refers to Laisnel de la Salle. The name *chole* may be connected with German *Kolbe*, and *golf* may be the form which this word would assume in a Celtic language. All this makes golf very old; but the question arises: are the 'holes' to which golfers play of Scotch or of Dutch origin? There are several old Flemish pictures of golf; do any of them show players in the act of 'holing out'? There is said to be such a picture at Neuchâtel.

A. LANG

I

Once upon a time there lived at the hamlet of Coq, near Condé-sur-l'Escaut, a wheelwright called Roger. He was a good fellow, untiring both at his sport and at his toil, and as skilful in lofting a ball with a stroke of his club as in putting together a cartwheel. Every one knows that the game of golf consists in driving towards a given point a ball of cherrywood with a club which has for head a sort of little iron shoe without a heel.

For my part, I do not know a more amusing game; and when the country is almost cleared of the harvest, men, women, children, everybody, drives his ball as you please, and there is nothing cheerier than to see them filing on a Sunday like a flight of starlings across potato-fields and ploughed lands.

II

Well, one Tuesday, it was a Shrove Tuesday, the wheelwright of Coq laid aside his plane, and was slipping on his blouse to go and drink his can of beer at Condé, when two strangers came in, club in hand.

'Would you put a new shaft to my club, master?' said one of them.

'What are you asking me, friends? A day like this! I wouldn't give the smallest stroke of the chisel for a brick of gold. Besides, does anyone play golf on Shrove Tuesday? You had much better go and see the mummers tumbling in the high street of Condé.'

'We take no interest in the tumbling of mummers,' replied the stranger. 'We have challenged each other at golf, and we want to play it out. Come, you won't refuse to help us, you who are said to be one of the finest players of the country?'

'If it is a match, that is different,' said Roger.

He turned up his sleeves, hooked on his apron, and in the twinkling of an eye had adjusted the shaft.

'How much do I owe you?' asked the unknown, drawing out his purse.

'Nothing at all, faith; it is not worthwhile.'

The stranger insisted, but in vain.

III

'You are too honest, i' faith,' said he to the wheelwright, 'for me to be in your debt. I will grant you the fulfilment of three wishes.'

'Don't forget to wish what is *best*,' added his companion.

At these words the wheelwright smiled incredulously.

'Are you not a couple of loafers of Capelette?' he asked, with a wink.

The idlers of the crossways of Capelette were considered the wildest wags in Condé.

'Whom do you take us for?' replied the unknown in a tone of severity, and with his club he touched an axle, made of iron, which instantly changed into one of pure silver.

'Who are you, then,' cried Roger, 'that your word is as good as ready money?'

'I am St Peter, and my companion is St Anthony, the patron of golfers.'

'Take the trouble to walk in, gentlemen,' said the wheel-wright of Coq; and he ushered the two saints into the back parlour. He offered them chairs, and went to draw a jug of beer in the cellar. They clinked their glasses together, and after each had lit his pipe –

'Since you are so good, sir saints,' said Roger, 'as to grant me the accomplishment of three wishes, know that for a long while I have desired three things. I wish, first of all, that whoever seats himself upon the elm-trunk at my door may not be able to rise without my permission. I like company, and it bores me to be always alone.'

St Peter shook his head, and St Anthony nudged his client.

IV

'When I play a game of cards, on Sunday evening, at the "Fighting Cock",' continued the wheelwright, 'it is no sooner nine o'clock than the garde-champêtre comes to chuck us out. I desire that whoever shall have his feet on my leathern apron cannot be driven from the place where I shall have spread it.'

St Peter shook his head, and St Anthony, with a solemn air, repeated –

'Don't forget what is *best*.'

'What is *best*,' replied the wheelwright of Coq nobly, 'is to be the first golfer in the world. Every time I find my master at golf it turns my blood as black as the inside of the chimney. So I want a club that will carry the ball as high as the belfry of Condé, and will infallibly win me my match.'

'So be it,' said St Peter.

'You would have done better,' said St Anthony, 'to have asked for your eternal salvation.'

'Bah!' replied the other. 'I have plenty of time to think of that; I am not yet greasing my boots for the long journey.'

The two saints went out, and Roger followed them, curious

to be present at such a rare game; but suddenly, near the Chapel of St Anthony, they disappeared.

The wheelwright then went to see the mummers tumbling in the high street of Condé.

When he returned, towards midnight, he found at the corner of his door the desired club. To his great surprise it was only a bad little iron head attached to a wretched worn-out shaft. Nevertheless he took the gift of St Peter and put it carefully away.

V

Next morning the Condéens scattered in crowds over the country, to play golf, eat red herrings, and drink beer, so as to scatter the fumes of wine from their heads, and to revive after the fatigues of the Carnival. The wheelwright of Coq came too, with his miserable club, and made such fine strokes that all the players left their games to see him play. The following Sunday he proved still more expert; little by little his fame spread through the land. From ten leagues round, the most skilful players hastened to come and be beaten, and it was then that he was named the Great Golfer.

He passed the whole Sunday in golfing, and in the evening he rested himself by playing a game of matrimony at the 'Fighting Cock'. He spread his apron under the feet of the players, and the devil himself could not have put them out of the tavern, much less the rural policeman. On Monday morning he stopped the pilgrims who were going to worship at Notre Dame de Bon Secours; he induced them to rest themselves upon his *causeuse*, and did not let them go before he had confessed them well.

In short, he led the most agreeable life that a good Fleming can imagine, and only regretted one thing – namely, that he had not wished it might last for ever.

VI

Well, it happened one day that the strongest player of Mons, who was called Paternostre, was found dead on the edge of a bunker. His head was broken, and near him was his niblick, red with blood.

They could not tell who had done his business, and as Paternostre often said that at golf he neither feared man nor devil, it occurred to them that he had challenged Mynheer van Belzébuth, and that as a punishment for this he had knocked him on the head. Mynheer van Belzébuth is, as every one knows, the greatest gamester that there is upon or under the earth, but the game he particularly affects is golf. When he goes his round in Flanders one always meets him, club in hand, like a true Fleming.

The wheelwright of Coq was very fond of Paternostre, who, next to himself, was the best golfer in the country. He went to his funeral with some golfers from the hamlets of Coq, La Cigogne, and La Queue de l'Ayache.

On returning from the cemetery they went to the tavern to drink, as they say, to the memory of the dead, and there they lost themselves in talk about the noble game of golf. When they separated, in the dusk of evening –

'A good journey to you,' said the Belgian players, 'and may St Anthony, the patron of golfers, preserve you from meeting the devil on the way!'

'What do I care for the devil?' replied Roger. 'If he challenged me I should soon beat him!'

The companions trotted from tavern to tavern without misadventure; but the wolf-bell had long tolled for retiring in the belfry of Condé when they returned each one to his own den.

VII

As he was putting the key into the lock the wheelwright thought he heard a shout of mocking laughter. He turned, and saw in the darkness a man six feet high, who again burst out laughing.

'What are you laughing at?' said he crossly.

'At what? Why, at the *aplomb* with which you boasted a little while ago that you would dare measure yourself against the devil.'

'Why not, if he challenged me?'

'Very well, my master, bring your clubs. I challenge you!' said Mynheer van Belzébuth, for it was himself. Roger recognised him by a certain odour of sulphur that always hangs about his majesty.

'What shall the stake be?' he asked resolutely.

'Your soul?'

'Against what?'

'Whatever you please.'

The wheelwright reflected.

'What have you there in your sack?'

'My spoils of the week.'

'Is the soul of Paternostre among them?'

'To be sure! and those of five other golfers; dead, like him, without confession.'

'I play you my soul against that of Paternostre.'

'Done!'

VIII

The two adversaries repaired to the adjoining field and chose for their goal the door of the cemetery of Condé.[1] Belzébuth teed a ball on a frozen heap, after which he said, according to custom –

'From here, as you lie, in how many turns of three strokes will you run in?'

'In two,' replied the great golfer.

And his adversary was not a little surprised, for from there to the cemetery was nearly a quarter of a league.

'But how shall we see the ball?' continued the wheelwright.

'True!' said Belzébuth.

He touched the ball with his club, and it shone suddenly in the dark like an immense glow-worm.

'Fore!' cried Roger.

He hit the ball with the head of his club, and it rose to the sky like a star going to rejoin its sisters. In three strokes it crossed three-quarters of the distance.

[1] They play to points, not holes.

'That is good!' said Belzébuth, whose astonishment redoubled. 'My turn to play now!'[2]

With one stroke of the club he drove the ball over the roofs of Coq nearly to Maison Blanche, half a league away. The blow was so violent that the iron struck fire against a pebble.

'Good St Anthony! I am lost, unless you come to my aid,' murmured the wheelwright of Coq.

He struck tremblingly; but though his arm was uncertain, the club seemed to have acquired a new vigour. At the second stroke the ball went as if of itself and hit the door of the cemetery.

'By the horns of my grandfather!' cried Belzébuth, 'it shall not be said that I have been beaten by a son of that fool Adam. Give me my revenge.'

'What shall we play for?'

'Your soul and that of Paternostre against the souls of two golfers.'

IX

The devil played up, 'pressing' furiously; his club blazed at each stroke with showers of sparks. The ball flew from Condé to Bon Secours, to Pernwelz, to Leuze. Once it spun away to Tournai, six leagues from there.

It left behind a luminous tail like a comet, and the two golfers followed, so to speak, on its track. Roger was never able to understand how he ran, or rather flew, so fast, and without fatigue.

In short, he did not lose a single game, and won the souls of the six defunct golfers. Belzébuth rolled his eyes like an angry tom-cat.

'Shall we go on?' said the wheelwright of Coq.

'No,' replied the other; 'they expect me at the Witches' Sabbath on the hill of Copiémont.'

'That brigand,' said he aside, 'is capable of filching all my game.'

---

[2] After each three strokes the opponent has one hit back, or into a hazard.

And he vanished.

Returned home, the Great Golfer shut up his souls in a sack and went to bed, enchanted to have beaten Mynheer van Belzébuth.

X

Two years after, the wheelwright of Coq received a visit which he little expected. An old man, tall, thin, and yellow, came into the workshop carrying a scythe on his shoulder.

'Are you bringing me your scythe to haft anew, master?'

'No, faith, *my* scythe is never unhafted.'

'Then how can I serve you?'

'By following me: your hour is come.'

'The devil!' said the great golfer, 'could you not wait a little till I have finished this wheel?'

'Be it so! I have done hard work today, and I have well earned a smoke.'

'In that case, master, sit down there on the *causeuse*. I have at your service some famous tobacco at seven petards the pound.'

'That's good, faith; make haste.'

And Death lit his pipe and seated himself at the door on the elm trunk.

Laughing in his sleeve, the wheelwright of Coq returned to his work. At the end of a quarter of an hour Death called to him –

'Ho! faith, will you soon have finished?'

The wheelwright turned a deaf ear and went on planing, singing –

> 'Attendez-moi sur l'orme;
> Vous m'attendrez longtemps.'

'I don't think he hears me,' said Death. 'Ho! friend, are you ready?'

> 'Va-t-en voir s'ils viennent, Jean,
> Va-t-en voir s'ils viennent,'

replied the singer.

'Would the brute laugh at me?' said Death to himself.

And he tried to rise.

To his great surprise he could not detach himself from the *causeuse*. He then understood he was the sport of a superior power.

'Let me see,' he said to Roger. 'What will you take to let me go? Do you wish me to prolong your life ten years?'

'J'ai de bon tabac dans ma tabatière,'

sang the Great Golfer.

'Will you take twenty years?'

'Il pleut, il pleut, bergère;
Rentre tes blancs moutons.'

'Will you take fifty, wheelwright? – may the devil admire you!'

The wheelwright of Coq intoned –

'Bon voyage, cher Dumollet,
A Saint-Malo débarquez sans naufrage.'

In the meanwhile the clock of Condé had just struck four, and the boys were coming out of school. The sight of this great dry heron of a creature who struggled on the *causeuse*, like a devil in a holy-water pot, surprised and soon delighted them.

Never suspecting that when seated at the door of the old, Death watches the young, they thought it funny to put their tongues at him, singing in chorus:

'Bon voyage, cher Dumollet,
A Saint-Malo débarquez sans naufrage.'

'Will you take a hundred years?' yelled Death.

'Hein? How? What? Were you not speaking of an extension of a hundred years? I accept with all my heart, master; but let us understand: I am not such a fool as to ask for the lengthening of my old age.'

'Then what do you want?'

'From old age I only ask the experience which it gives by degrees. "Si jeunesse savait, si vieillesse pouvait!" says the proverb. I wish to preserve for a hundred years the strength of a young man, and to acquire the experience of an old one.'

'So be it,' said Death; 'I shall return this day a hundred years.'

> 'Bon voyage, cher Dumollet,
> A Saint-Malo débarquez sans naufrage.'

XI

The Great Golfer began a new life. At first he enjoyed perfect happiness, which was increased by the certainty of its not ending for a hundred years. Thanks to his experience, he so well understood the management of his affairs that he could leave his mallet and shut up shop.

He experienced, nevertheless, an annoyance he had not foreseen. His wonderful skill at golf ended by frightening the players whom he had at first delighted, and was the cause of his never finding anyone who would play against him.

He therefore quitted the canton and set out on his travels over French Flanders, Belgium, and all the greens where the noble game is held in honour. At the end of twenty years he returned to Coq to be admired by a new generation of golfers, after which he departed to return twenty years later.

Alas! In spite of its apparent charm, this existence before long became a burden to him. Besides that, it bored him to win on every occasion; he was tired of passing like the Wandering Jew through generations, and of seeing the sons, grandsons, and great-grandsons of his friends grow old and die out. He was constantly reduced to making new friendships which were undone by the age or death of his fellows; all changed around him, he only did not change.

He grew impatient of this eternal youthfulness, which condemned him to taste the same pleasures for ever, and he sometimes longed to know the calmer joys of old age. One day he caught himself at his looking-glass, examining whether his hair had not begun to grow white; nothing seemed so beautiful to him now as the snow on the forehead of the old.

XII

In addition to this, experience soon made him so wise that he was no longer amused at anything. If sometimes in the tavern he had a fancy for making use of his apron to pass the night at cards: 'What is the good of this excess?' whispered experience; 'it is not sufficient to be unable to shorten one's days, one must also avoid making one's-self ill.'

He reached the point of refusing himself the pleasure of drinking his pint and smoking his pipe. Why, indeed, plunge into dissipations which enervate the body and dull the brain?

The wretch went further, and gave up golf! Experience convinced him that the game is a dangerous one, which overheats one and is eminently adapted to produce colds, catarrhs, rheumatism, and inflammation of the lungs.

Besides, what is the use, and what great glory is it to be reputed the first golfer in the world?

Of what use is glory itself? A vain hope, vain as the smoke of a pipe.

When experience had thus bereft him one by one of his delusions, the unhappy golfer became mortally weary. He saw that he had deceived himself, that delusion has its price, and that the greatest charm of youth is perhaps its inexperience.

He thus arrived at the term agreed on in the contract, and as he had not had a paradise here below, he sought through his hardly-acquired wisdom a clever way of conquering one above.

XIII

Death found him at Coq at work in his shop. Experience had at least taught him that work is the most lasting of pleasures.

'Are you ready?' said Death.

'I am.'

He took his club, put a score of balls in his pocket, threw his sack over his shoulder, and buckled his gaiters without taking off his apron.

'What do you want your club for?'

'Why, to golf in paradise with my patron St Anthony.

'Do you fancy, then, that I am going to conduct you to paradise?'

'You must, as I have half a dozen souls to carry there that I once saved from the clutches of Belzébuth.'

'Better have saved your own. *En route, cher Dumollet!*'

The Great Golfer saw that the Old Reaper bore him a grudge, and that he was going to conduct him to the paradise of the lost.

Indeed, a quarter of an hour later the two travellers knocked at the gate of hell.

'Toc, toc!'

'Who is there?'

'The wheelwright of Coq,' said the Great Golfer.

'Don't open the door,' cried Belzébuth; 'that rascal wins at every turn; he is capable of depopulating my empire.'

Roger laughed in his sleeve.

'Oh! you are not saved,' said Death. 'I am going to take you where you won't be cold either.'

Quicker than a beggar would have emptied a poorbox they were in purgatory.

'Toc, toc!'

'Who is there?'

'The wheelwright of Coq,' said the Great Golfer.

'But he is in a state of mortal sin,' cried the angel on duty. 'Take him away from here – he can't come in.'

'I cannot, all the same, let him linger between heaven and earth,' said Death; 'I shall shunt him back to Coq.'

'Where they will take me for a ghost. Thank you! Is there not still paradise?'

XIV

They were there at the end of a short hour.

'Toc, toc!'

'Who is there?'

'The wheelwright of Coq,' said the Great Golfer.

'Ah! my lad,' said St Peter half opening the door, 'I am really grieved. St Anthony told you long ago you had better ask for the salvation of your soul.'

'That is true, St Peter,' replied Roger with a sheepish air. 'And how is he, that blessed St Anthony? Could I not come in for one moment to return the visit he once paid me?'

'Why, here he comes,' said St Peter, throwing the door wide open.

In the twinkling of an eye the sly golfer had flung himself into paradise, unhooked his apron, let it fall to the ground, and seated himself down on it.

'Good morning, St Anthony,' said he with a fine salute. 'You see I had plenty of time to think of paradise, for here we are!'

'What! *You* here!' cried St Anthony.

'Yes, I and my company,' replied Roger, opening his sack and scattering on the carpet the souls of six golfers.

'Will you have the goodness to pack right off, all of you?'

'Impossible!' said the Great Golfer, showing his apron.

'The rogue has made game of us,' said St Anthony. 'Come, St Peter, in memory of our game of golf, let him in with his souls. Besides, he has had his purgatory on earth.'

'It is not a very good precedent,' murmured St Peter.

'Bah!' replied Roger, 'if we have a few good golfers in paradise, where is the harm?'

XV

Thus, after having lived long, golfed much, and drunk many cans of beer, the wheelwright of Coq called the Great Golfer was admitted to paradise; but I advise no one to copy him, for it is not quite the right way to go, and St Peter might not always be so compliant, though great allowances must be made for golfers.

4

A BRAID HILLS MYSTERY

by J.M. Barrie

THE first journal to regularly publish short stories about golf was the famous *Blackwood's Magazine*, whose editor John Blackwood was a keen golfer and had actually bought himself a house close to St. Andrews. In time, this property, called 'Strathtyrum', became a kind of magnet for all the magazine's contributors who loved playing the game. According to Horace Hutchinson, "Thither, about the year 1880, resorted all men eminent in Scottish literature and far beyond. Golf, rather than literature, was the household word, and the men of letters wrote about golf in *Maga*.'

Pre-eminent among these writers was J. M. Barrie, later to become famous as a novelist, dramatist and creator of the immortal Peter Pan. Barrie took up golf while at Edinburgh University, and though never more than a competent player was sufficiently interested in the game to write several magazine and newspaper stories which, curiously, have never been collected. (As a matter of record, cricket was Barrie's first sporting love – strange for a Scotsman, perhaps – and he founded and captained his own team, Allahakbarries CC, for which a number of his literary friends played, including Sir Arthur Conan Doyle.)

Barrie's golfing stories are all about the kind of characters that the game attracts, but I doubt if there is an odder one than the central figure in 'A Braid Hills Mystery'. For those not familiar with Scotland, Braid Hills is a public course in the neighbourhood of Edinburgh.

A BRAID HILLS MYSTERY

Stubble Row is one of the arms which Edinburgh stretches out toward the Braid Hills, but though the tenements have been finished for eighteen months or more, a number of them are still standing empty. Fourteen and Sixteen, adjoining houses, are occupied, the former by a gentleman of unknown occupation, whose recent accession to fortune has greatly puzzled his neighbour at No. Sixteen. Until lately his impecuniosity was so notorious as to be the subject of commiseration with all his neighbours, and the tradesmen with whom he deals never met him without making pointed allusions to 'that pound note', which it seems to have been his occupation to borrow here and there. His great-coat had also been seen by the curious in a High Street window, and reports said that his furniture had gone to the pawn shop, a chair at a time. There was no other such needy person in Stubble Row, and No. Fourteen admitted it himself. Suddenly, however, his fortune seemed to change, and instead of going out of his house, furniture began to go in. At the same time he became secretive, presenting, as No. Sixteen complained, the appearance of a man who had discovered a new way of making money, and meant to keep it to himself.

The change at No. Fourteen was first discovered by No. Sixteen (who is a lady) one morning when she saw a dozen bottles of beer delivered at No. Fourteen's door. She ran round to No. Nine to say that Fourteen had got the better of another grocer, and they spent (as has since been admitted) half an hour in discussing the amount of whistling the grocer would have to go through before he saw his money. Later in the day, Sixteen was extremely disgusted to see Fourteen ostentatiously drinking beer in his back-garden, which is the exact size of a billiard table, but not the same colour. Fourteen sat on a garden chair – which looked new – with his feet resting on a clothes basket; and, while Sixteen looked on, congratulating herself that she was not as her neighbour, he accidentally knocked over the beer bottle, and broke it. Had the same thing happened to her, she would have bewailed the extra expense thus entailed; but her neighbour, who was reputed without a penny to bless himself with, laughed genially, and then flung the broken bottle over the wall into her garden. His impudence staggered her, but she picked up the pieces, meaning to return them to him at once, when she had the presence of mind to stay her hand and glance at the bottle to see what grocer's label was on it. Discovering that it had been bottled by Simpson, of the neighbourhood, whose teas will well repay a trial, if what you want is fragance combined with economy (see handbills), she thought it her duty as a Christian to look in at Simpson's the first time she passed that way, and warn him against having any further dealings with No. Fourteen. The grocer, with whom she does not deal except for American cheese, which is one of his specialties, but not so remunerative as tea, received her curtly, and said that Fourteen's beer had been paid for, money down. He also hinted that if she thought more of her own affairs, and less of her neighbour's, she would keep her doorsteps cleaner, and she left the shop, resolved never again to do a good turn for anybody.

Had Fourteen now lapsed into his former condition of impecuniosity, Sixteen (though reluctant to think ill of any one) would have concluded that he had merely paid for the beer in order to make a good impression, and so pave the way for running up an account at Simpson's. But a few days afterwards he was seen walking down the street under a new umbrella, and even while Sixteen was wondering with Nine whether he had got a present of it, or bought it when the shopman was not looking, a rumour spread through Stubble Row that fourteen had been in at the butcher's and paid his long-standing account for £1, 12s. 7d. Sixteen flung on her cloak and hurried to the butcher's, where the story was confirmed. The general excitement reached its height on the 12th of last month, when a piano was delivered at Sixteen's door. Inquiries were at once instituted, when it was found that the piano had been taken on the three years' hire system, and that Sixteen had paid for a month in advance.

All this time, while the neighbourhood was thinking him over, No. Fourteen was going about as usual. Sixteen was so annoyed at her failure to unravel the mystery that she invited him to tea; but though he accepted the invitation, and both ate and drank heartily, she could get nothing out of him. He admitted that his affairs had taken a turn for the better, but beyond that remained stubbornly silent. Hitherto the chief cause of his poverty had been a disinclination to work, and it was noticed that he was still as idle as ever. He spent his days smoking in the back-garden or strolling about the streets. The only conclusion to come to, therefore, was that someone had left him money. Certain of Fourteen's male neighbours disagreed with this view however, their ground being that, when in the public at the end of the street, Fourteen occasionally let drop hints of a new profession he had invented. He was very 'close' as to what it was, but they gathered that he followed it in the night time. Probably this was a mere surmise, a deduction from the fact that he obviously did nothing during the day.

Sixteen admitted that there might be something in this theory, and was finally converted to it. Her conversion dates from the afternoon when she saw Fourteen leave his house with a heavy bag on his shoulders. It was about the size, she said, of a pillowcase and she was made suspicious by his evident anxiety not to be followed. She hurriedly put on her bonnet and ran after him. At the corner of the street, however, he was lost to view. This happened on a Monday, and on the following Monday the incident was repeated, but later in the evening.

Sixteen and Nine were at the former's window by four o'clock in the afternoon on the third Monday, resolved not to quit their post until they had solved the mystery. They waited nearly four hours before Fourteen came out. He had no bag on his shoulders this time, and they feared that their watch had been in vain. He walked down the street, and they opened the window to crane their necks after him. Their surprise was considerable when he was seen hailing a cab. Cabs are seldom hailed in Stubble Row, except by mischievous boys. Fourteen walked alongside the cab to his house, which he entered, after first directing the cabman to wait. The excitement at No. Sixteen was now such that No. Nine hit her head on the windowsill and did not know it for some time afterwards. In a minute Fourteen emerged, staggering under the weight of a heavy sack. He put this into the cab, and drove off.

Sixteen and Nine sat looking at each other, and then had a glass of sherry in a cup. They were both rather frightened, and to this day neither can say which was the first to mention Burke and Hare. Horrible though it seemed, Fourteen was behaving in a manner that quite suggested these notorious criminals. They conveyed the bodies of the murdered persons in a sack, and sometimes they had the audacity to use conveyances. It was in the night time that they pursued their horrid calling. The more sherry Sixteen and Nine drank the more certain they felt that the case should be put into the hands of the police.

Against Sixteen's advice, Nine first told her husband of the discovery, and he did not receive her plan of action favourably. He said he would black her eye if she told tales on her neighbour. Other persons saw their duty more clearly than Nine's husband, and a meeting was held, at which they agreed to catch Fourteen red-handed on the following Monday. The local policeman pooh-poohed their suspicions, but undertook to be on the spot.

Fourteen was caught in the street with a heavy bag on his shoulders. The weight of the bag is best known to No. Four, whom it caught in the small of the back. There was a fierce struggle, which was only ended by the intervention of the policeman. Fourteen would not deliver up his bag until told that he would otherwise be given in charge. He then consented to divulge the contents to the policeman's eyes alone. There was an outcry against this, but the policeman assented, and to the rage of Fourteen's captors the door of Fourteen's house was closed against them.

The policeman has admitted that Fourteen attempted to bribe him, but, of course, he indignantly rejected all offers. The bag was then opened, when, to the bewilderment of the officer of the law, it was found to be full of golf balls. Fourteen subsequently made the following statement:–

'It is quite true that until lately I was in very impecunious circumstances. This would not have troubled me had not my creditors taken it so much to heart. Their conversation was eternally on the one subject, and I found it tedious. Had I been able to work without exerting myself, I would gladly had embraced some trade. Unfortunately there are different laws for the rich and poor.

'I think it is only two months ago since an accident made a material difference in my circumstances. I had gone for a walk on the Braid Hills. It was a fine afternoon. A great number of golfers were engaged in play. I am not a golfer. It seems to me to be hard work. I was strolling in the long grass around the course, when my foot struck against something hard. I picked it up. It was a golf ball. A hundred yards further on I found another ball, then another. I did not know what was the value of these balls; but being anxious to make an honest living, I took them to a shop. I was surprised at the handsome price I got for them.

'Early next morning, before the golfers were out, I returned to the Braid Hills, and made a search for golf balls. I found seven. From that day I saw that I had a career before me. Every morning, while most of the citizens were sleeping, I was out on the Braid Hills pursuing my vocation. My finds varied in number, and some days I was unlucky; but, on the whole, as my skill increased, the profession became more and more remunerative. I invented one implement for picking golf balls out of long grass, and another for getting at the roots of whins. My great day was Sunday, partly because it gave me longer time to search, but mainly because Saturday is the chief day of the week for golf. Many matches take place on Saturday too. Every Monday I sold my golf balls to a firm of makers.

'My reason for keeping this a secret is that, if the new calling was generally known, I would have rivals in it. It could keep some more of us, no doubt, in comfort, but there would be a rush of needy persons. If I could have bought the monopoly I would gladly have done so, for then I could have extended my business. Instead of looking for the golf balls myself, I would have paid boys a small wage to bring them to me.

'It is only now that I realise what an excellent sport golf is. Formerly, I thought it too hard work for anybody. Of late, however, I have become quite an enthusiast. I do not play myself, but I advise all others to do so. I spend great part of my days now recommending the young to play golf, because it is a fine, healthy pastime, and the old because it gives them an appetite. I am also thoroughly of opinion that ladies should play golf. My advice is that the Braid Hills should be chosen for playing on. It is a splendid course, and I am always delighted when I see the newspapers cracking it up. I don't agree, however, with the view that the whins and grass should be cut down. That would put an end to the industry I now follow, and would naturally lessen my interest in the noble and ancient game.'

5

THE CULBIN GAME

by C. L. Graves & E. V. Lucas

IF *Blackwood's* was Scotland's leading magazine for golfing stories, *Punch* could lay claim to the title in England. As early as the turn of the century, the famous humour magazine was making gentle fun at the expense of the game and its players. Two of the magazine's best-known contributors at this time were the inventive comic writer, C. L. Graves, and E. V. Lucas, a prolific essayist and anthologiser who was also the magazine's assistant editor for a number of years. Both men enjoyed golf, and their keen eye as observers and sense of humour produced a whole string of stories such as 'Illustrious Golfers' (November 1907) – about the Shah of Persia and the Dowager Empress of China 'the most remarkable of female golfers east of Suez' – to 'Aero Golf' (December 1909) which contained a proposal to utilise model aeroplanes in the search for missing balls!

A character who featured in several of the Graves–Lucas contributions was a redoubtable old Scottish professional called Archie McLurkin, who also turns up in the following selection. 'Gossip From The Links by Johnny L. Hutchings' (August 1904) is intended as a kind of spoof of the golfing commentators – Horace Hutchinson, being the man most obviously in mind – who were then appearing in increasing numbers in newspaper and magazine columns. I hope, though, that when the reader has met McLurkin he will agree that a collection of the best of the stories about this ingenious character is long overdue . . .

THE CULBIN GAME

GOSSIP FROM THE LINKS

By Johnny L. Hutchings

I have recently spent a week on the Culbin Sands Links, about 10 miles from Nairn, a course of such unprecedented and peculiar texture and character that it has caused me to revise, if not actually to revolutionise, a great many of my views on the subject of driving, approaching and putting. The Culbin Sands, as readers of St John's *Wild Sports of the Highlands* are well aware, lie between the fertile plains of Moray and the shores of the Moray Firth, and consist of a stretch of sandhills, in most parts formed of pure and very fine yellowish sand, without a blade of vegetation of any description, and constantly shifting and changing their shape and appearance on the recurrence of continued dry winds.

Westwards, towards Nairn, the sandhills are interrupted by

an extent of broken hillocks, covered with the deepest heather imaginable, which conceals innumerable pits and holes, many of the latter not above a foot in diameter, but three or four feet deep, and so completely concealed by the growth of moss and heather as to form the most perfect traps for golf balls and golfers that were ever devised. Throughout the whole tract of this wild ground there are large numbers of foxes, which grow to a great size, feeding during the season on young roe, wild ducks and black game, and when these fail they make great havoc amongst the Springvale Hawks, Kempshall Arlingtons, and other rubber-covered denizens of the adjoining country.

No greens being available and the links being of the nature of one continuous hazard, an entirely new phase of the game has been evolved by the ingenuity of the residents, amongst whom the palm must be awarded to Archie McLurkin, the local professional and keeper of the bunkers, under whose auspices I have been instructed in the niceties of the Culbin game.

Perhaps the best idea of the novelty of the game may be gained from the statement that not a single club of normal pattern is of the slightest use on the Culbin Links. McLurkin's clubs are not merely unlike any that I have ever set eyes on in England or America, but they have special names of their own. For striking off from the tee he employs a weapon called a mid-bilger, with an enormously long shaft and a head resembling that of a niblick, as the tees, like most of the course, consist of extremely fine and loose sand. For playing through the green – if such a term can be used – he employs a waffle, a club with a very 'whippy' shaft and a soft, rather spongy head, made of compressed seaweed with a leaden face. With a gale of wind behind him, he can sometimes hit the ball with the waffle about sixty or seventy yards, but I never succeeded in sending it more than about half that distance. For approaching he generally uses the sclaffy, a short iron club with a head shaped rather like a seltzer-water bottle, but when the ball is barely visible he takes his delver, which resembles the spade used in cutting peats, and literally shovels the ball out of its lair.

[53]

As in no circumstances whatever does the ball run more than three or four inches, putting is impossible, and the place of the hole is taken by a stick, as in croquet. But I have omitted to mention the most characteristic of all the Culbin clubs – that employed in extricating the ball from the deep pits in the heather described in my first paragraph. For this, McLurkin, who is a bit of a mechanic, has devised an implement which he calls the diver, which is nothing else than an air-pump by means of which he is able to blow the ball out of a hole four feet deep. The rules for the use of the diver, or flimp, as the caddies call it, are rather complicated, but it may suffice to say that the player is allowed to blow once without loss. I have also omitted to mention that, in order to prevent the player sinking in the sand, he is obliged to don footgear somewhat resembling the *ski* of the Norwegians. Altogether it is a most fascinating, if somewhat fatiguing game, and as a means of obtaining a mastery of the short duffing shot I know nothing to equal it.

But there are other advantages connected with the Culbin game which it would not be right to overlook. The complete absence of turf renders it impossible for even the worst player to do the slightest damage to the course. There is never any need to replace divots, because divots do not exist. Again, the game being entirely a question of 'carry' and not 'run', the burning question of stymies is practically eliminated. The greens are never too keen or fiery, and owing to the practically limitless extent of the Culbin sandhills – estimated at about 25 square miles – there is not the slightest risk of the course needing a rest: in fact, the greater the drought the more interesting is the condition of the links. A low score, however, is impossible at all times. McLurkin's record is 253, and I am free to confess that my first round took me something over 700 strokes.

McLurkin is very anxious that the next Open Championship meeting should be held on the Culbin Sands Links, but the leading professionals whom I have consulted are by no means favourable to the proposal. Indeed Andrew Kirkaldy waxed positively lyrical in his indignation. 'We're not Arabians,' he said, in that picturesque style for which he is so justly celebrated,'to go smothering ourselves in that blooming Sahara just to please McLurkin,' and Old Tom cordially endorsed his view. Still, from a geological and psychological point of view, there is a good deal to be said in favour of the change of venue, and I may perhaps return to the subject in the near future. Next week, however, I must devote the space at my disposal to the more urgent question of the use of sedatives, and in particular of phenacetin, in match-play on links where the air is over-stimulating, and so calculated to disturb the nerves of the highly strung golfer.

6

COLONEL BELCHER'S GHOST STORY

by Henry Leach

I T was inevitable that the rapid rise in the popularity of golf in the early years of the twentieth century should result in the creation of magazines specifically devoted to the sport. One of the first of these was *The Golfer*, founded and edited for many years by the next contributor, Henry Leach. Devoted to the game since his childhood, Leach had begun writing about golf while still in his teens and was a respected contributor to a number of newspapers and journals by the time he was in his thirties. When his mail began to bring him increasing proof of the obviously strong interest in golf among his readers, he decided to launch *The Golfer* to cater specifically to their need for information, instruction and entertainment.

Henry Leach wrote numerous articles and stories for his magazine, including the long-running series, 'Letters of a Modern Golfer to his Grandfather' in which a young player informed his older relative of all the changes that were taking place in the game. These letters were published in book form in 1910. Leach also demonstrated his wholehearted enthusiasm for the game in other works such as *The Spirit of the Links* (1907) and *The Happy Golfer* (1914). He particularly enjoyed recounting golfers' tall stories about their alleged achievements on the links, and my favourite among such yarns is 'Colonel Belcher's Ghost Story' which first appeared in *The Golfer* in 1910.

FORE!

COLONEL BELCHER'S GHOST STORY

Our own little set of golfers assembled together yesterday for a last day before breaking up. We thought it would be a good thing to have a kind of reunion in the club-house before going home and scattering outselves in diverse directions for the Christmas holidays, and we arranged it. I had polished off Charlie Spink at the fifteenth hole, and some of the other games having also ended a little way from the home green, it happened that we were all squatted in the warmth of the big fire in the smoke-room in good time, except Colonel Belcher and Herbert Watson, who, having large stakes on their match, fought to a finish in what they conceived at the time to be the good old-fashioned way, and so went to the twenty-first hole, where the Colonel was enabled to rejoice.

'Now, boys,' said he, on joining us, 'we must enjoy some moments of the proper Christmas sort of happiness before we depart. Mellor, touch that bell and and get the boy to coal up the fire, and then if you don't mind I will constitute myself chairman for the occasion, and make some special Christmas golfing drinks, something like those we used to get for ourselves in the old times when golf was really golf, but for all that was not any better than the thing we have in these days, despite what some may say.'

Charles Spink made an observation to the effect that the only time that what was described as a Christmas golfing drink had been submitted to his experienced palate, he found it distinctly suggestive of rubber-cored balls boiled down in methylated spirits. The Colonel departed for a short season for conference with the steward, and presently returned with a large steaming bowl, which was deposited on the floor amidst us, and from which each man partook according to his desire. It was excellent, and, as Harry Bryant said, it produced an effect which seemed peculiarly suitable to the moment.

Silence was then demanded for the golfing ghost story that Belcher had promised to relate.

'I daresay some of you boys have heard,' he began, 'of my elder brother, Sir James Belcher, who plays no golf, but lives a very fair sporting sort of life out at Gloomsby Castle. Well, though he plays no golf, as I have just said, there was once a six-hole course laid out in the park, but it might be hard now to trace anything of it except one or two of the teeing grounds and one big bunker and a pond behind it, for it has not been used for more than thirty years. Fact is, the old castle's haunted, and that golf course had something to do with it, and so gradually it got left alone.

'Gloomsby, you see, and the title came along to James from our uncle, old Sir Walter Belcher, who was a real sport and quite an excellent fellow in many ways. When he was getting very well on in years, and was beginning to have to give up things (by the way, he was an old bachelor then), he took up what they told him was an old man's game, and he had this six-hole course made for himself.

'A most extraordinary thing happened soon afterwards. A young girl, a Miss Dorothy Blessington, was creating some sort of sensation in those parts just then, not merely by her beauty, charm of manner, and general attractiveness, but by the remarkable feats of sportsmanship which she was performing almost daily. She was just a champion at everything, every game that a woman could play at, and some that other women couldn't or didn't. She was the finest rider to hounds in the whole country. How it came about nobody ever quite knew, but some attachment undoubtedly sprang up between May and December; May being this sporting Dolly, and December old Sir Walter, and before we had ceased rubbing our eyes in surprise they were married! She was nineteen, and he was sixty-seven.'

'It is often a very good arrangement,' Herbert Watson murmured pensively.

'Very likely,' Belcher assented. 'They seemed very happy together, and apparently were having quite a good time. Sir Walter took a new lease of youth, and was as sprightly as ever; but still at every form of exercise or sport that they took part in together his young wife would beat him, and was proud to do so – every form but one.

'He taught her golf, and when he did so he had one or two alterations made to the course. He was out for business this time. He had a high mound thrown up a hundred and forty yards from the third tee, from which it had to be carried – gutty days, mind you. Not only that, but the old villain had a pond thirty feet wide dug on the other side, so that the player had to make his ball do a kind of Grand National hidden water jump. It is the most hateful form of bunker that I know. You think you're over and safe, and you're not. Like the eighth, Hades, at Sandwich, you know.

'Well, boys, old Sir Walter taught the Royal and Ancient game to this prize wife of his, and she soon showed good form. She did the Taylor kind of pitches by instinct, and drove a wonderful ball. She quickly realised the pleasure and the merit of long driving, and Sir Walter, who used to talk very patronisingly to her when they were at their golf, said that, of course, driving was a fine thing, but not everything. However, before she could consider herself at all proficient she must be able, so he told her, to drive the bunker and pond at the third hole. But though she could often clear the mound she could never give her ball that little bit extra which would have enabled it to get over the water. Seeing it skimming past the guide-post on the bunker, she would turn sideways and listen intently, and a moment later the faint sound of a splash told her than one more ball had gone to the bottom.

'Sir Walter insisted that she must try, try, try again, and perhaps after all some day she might do it as easily as he did. Note, the old boy carefully refrained from displaying his greatness at this hole in practice; but somehow, when they played serious matches together, which they did twice a week, uncle Walter *always drove the bunker and water*, and got his ball on the green, and Lady Belcher was *always in*! He used to send his caddie forward to perch himself on top of the mound and signal what happened, and when the boy always indicated that the one ball was over and the other in, she gradually became very, very sore about it and very disconsolate. She always played the last three holes badly after losing the third, and always lost the match, and she didn't like being beaten by her husband in this manner.

'The people round about said that a change came over her, that she lost most of her spirits, and did not take the same interest in things that she used to do. She gave up the golf at last, admitting herself beaten, and she abandoned other things soon afterwards.

'In the following winter she was taken ill, and on Christmas Eve, being then in a delirious fever, during the temporary absence of the nurse told off to watch her, she rose from her bed, put on a dressing-gown, stole quietly downstairs, let herself out of the house, and ran down the park – to the third hole! Here she stood for a moment on the top of the bunker – they had missed her from her room and were now running after her – plainly to be seen in the bright moonlight, and then with a piercing scream she threw herself into the icy water!'

'Bless my soul!' gasped Teddy Masters. 'And what then, Belcher, old boy? – what then?'

'The nurses, servants, and old Sir Walter himself were all at the waterside a moment later,' the Colonel went on in subdued tones and slowly, 'and in the old man dashed and spluttered and brought his poor suffering lady out. But she could not recover from such a shock. She died before morning. Two months later Sir Walter shut up Gloomsby and went abroad, but he also died a year afterwards, and they say he never played any game or dined in any company again from the day of his wife's death.

'The ghost? Well, if you can get my respected brother to ask you over to his place for a few days, tell him you have no silly superstitions and don't mind if you do take on the haunted room. Then, somewhere between one and two in the morning you will be awakened by a moaning, and you will see a white, filmy lady in the room in the attitude of a golfer preparing to drive. She has a fine style, takes a full, free swing, finishes with a follow through which is quite divine, and then waits a moment listening. And then she wails in agony, "I – n again! I – n again!' and disappears. An odd thing is that the ghost only appears to real golfers".

We all of us thought this was a very good ghost tale indeed, and thanked the Colonel effusively; but Norman Carson said there was one point that he was not satisfied about, and that was how was it that old Sir Walter always did that very long carry himself when nobody would really expect him to do anything of the kind?

'Ah, yes, that's it!' the Colonel answered. 'Some people say that in the explanation of that lies the *raison d'être* of the ghost. We in the family are rather shy of discussing this part of the story, and I will only just tell you what the suggested explanation is, on condition that you never refer to the matter again. Well, in a word, it is said – only said, mind you – that Uncle Walter *never once did carry the water*, but by not going for it he made certain of clearing the ridge, and – well, his caddie did the rest – just dropped another ball like his master's on the fairway. After the tragedy Sir Walter packed the boy off to the West Indies.'

7

A ONE-BALL MATCH

by Gerald Batchelor

ANOTHER prolific contributor to the early golf magazines was
Gerald Batchelor, whose lively style and evident appreciation
and love of the game can be found in publications such as
Golf Illustrated, The World of Golf, The Golf Monthly and
Golfing. For many years up to the outbreak of the Second
World War his name was among the most popular of all golf
writers.

Like Henry Leach, Batchelor loved the game's characters,
and in one of his best-known books, *Golf Stories* (1935),
drew this amusing comparison between certain players and
the animal world. 'Some of the animals,' he wrote, 'would,
unfortunately, be rather unpopular in the club-house, for who
would care to pal up with the long-tailed tit, the lyre bird, the
badger, the boar, the grouse, the puff-adder, the cheetah, the
carp or the bear (with a sore head)? And on the ladies' course
we should find the spoonbill and possibly the shrew. The
wry-neck would be noticed on the green, and all the game
birds would certainly be bittern with the sport!'

It is not easy to pick the best from among Gerald Batchelor's many humorous stories, but I have finally settled for the
following delightful yarn of the impoverished golfer Clerkson
and how he solved the problems of loosing too many of his
balls. . .

A ONE-BALL MATCH

It was the first day of Spring and I arrived early on the links, eager to make the most of my holiday.

I found a solitary figure in the smoking-room, poring over the latest book on golf, and recognised him as a fellow member whom I knew to be a good golfer, a good sportsman, and one of the pleasantest men in the Club.

Clerkson had retired early from Government service owing to ill-health, and it was understood that, in spite of being an unmarried man, he possessed hardly sufficient means to be able to afford the luxury of playing golf regularly.

'Hullo, Clerkson!' I said, 'I haven't seen you here for ages. Have you been away?'

'No,' he replied, 'I – er – I've given up golf.'

'Given up golf?' I repeated in amazement, '*you*, the keenest player in all –, but you've been ill, perhaps?'

'Yes, I have,' he said, 'but that is not the real reason. The fact is, I found the game too expensive. I don't complain of my limited income – it is nobody's business but my own – but I don't mind telling you that many a time when I have played here and lost a ball I have been forced to economise by going without my lunch!

'Now you will understand why I have always been so

anxious to avail myself of the full five minutes allowed for search, however hopeless the case might appear. It's my own fault for ever taking up golf. I wish I hadn't. No, I don't wish that, and I would willingly deny myself anything rather than be compelled to give it up.

'The limit came when they put up the price of balls. That extra sixpence meant everything to me, you see, so I had no choice but to depart from my earthly paradise.

'I thought I could do it, too, but I was wrong. The exercise of brain and muscle, so happily combined, had become as necessary to me as food and sleep.

'My health began to suffer. Doctors could do nothing. They failed to diagnose my case. I got worse and worse, until I was almost given up.

'This morning I took the matter out of their hands, for I had thought of a plan. I jumped out of bed, enjoyed a big breakfast, and hurried up to the links. I feel better already.'

'Excellent!' I exclaimed, 'will you have a match?'

'I should be ashamed to ask you to play with me,' he replied, 'for I'm afraid I might spoil your game.'

'What do you mean?' I asked. 'You are a better golfer than I am.'

'Ah, but I fear you do not quite understand the conditions under which I am compelled to play,' he said; 'in future I shall always have to play *without a ball!*'

'Without a ball?' I repeated; 'you are surely joking. How is it possible?'

'Well, if you really don't object to watching the experiment,' said Clerkson, 'I will show you.'

'Perhaps you will remember,' he continued, as we made for the first tee, 'that it is my custom to take a trial swing before every drive? It was this which suggested the idea. I was always able to judge fairly accurately by the feeling of the swing whether the stroke would have been successful. Will you take the honour?'

'Shall we have a ball on?' I asked as usual, forgetting for the moment the peculiar conditions of the coming match. Clerkson seemed to be engaged in a mental struggle. Then he answered 'Yes!'

I made a fair drive and stood aside to see what my opponent would do. He took some sand, pinched it into a tee, addressed it carefully, and played.

'Ah!' he exclaimed: 'I was afraid I should slice. I must have been standing that way.'

He made off towards the rough, where I saw him play two strokes, and we walked on together to my ball. I also played two more shots before reaching the green.

'Where are you?' I asked.

'Didn't you see it?' said Clerkson. 'I was rather surprised that you did not compliment me on the stroke. It was a wicked lie.'

'Are you – are you near the hole?' I inquired, as I settled down to a long putt.

'I don't see it at present,' he replied, looking about, 'I hope it hasn't run over. Good Heavens!' he went on, as he reached the pin. 'It's *in the hole!*'

He stooped and seemed to pick it out.

'I really must apologise for that fluke,' my opponent said, as we walked to the next tee, 'but I knew it was a fine shot directly I had played it, and I thought it deserved to be pretty close.'

'It looks as if this is going to be rather a one-sided match,' I said to myself, as I watched him dispatch what he described as a 'screamer', and I began to wonder whether Clerkson had planned this game in order to provide himself with the necessary ball. Knowing him to be a thoroughly good fellow, however, I dismissed the suspicion from my mind.

These misgivings prevented me from concentrating my attention entirely on the game, with the result that I played very indifferently and reached the second green three strokes to the bad. After I had holed my putt, Clerkson kept walking up and down the green in his attempts to get into the hole.

'Your hole!' he cried at last; 'putting was always my weak point.'

The game continued to be very even. If I obtained a lead of one hole my opponent invariably seemed to hit a tremendous distance from the next tee. At the fourth he played a shot which must easily have beaten the record drive. On the other hand, if he happened to become one up he lost the next by taking three or four putts.

At the sixth hole his ball disappeared into a gorse bush. Formerly he would have been much disturbed by such an occurrence, but now he seemed to accept the situation with philosophic calm.

'Come along; never mind,' he said, after a casual look round; 'it's of no consequence; only an old gutta, you know. I'll drop another' – which he did. He must have lost quite half a dozen balls during the round.

At the ninth we were all square. I was beginning to find my game better now.

'Mark it!' cried Clerkson, directly after driving from the tenth tee; 'I've lost it in the sun.'

'I see it,' I said; 'you've pulled it rather badly, I'm afraid, and it has landed in "Purgatory" bunker.' I pointed out to him that it was lying in a hopeless position, and he gave up the hole.

At the twelfth hole Clerkson made a very serious error of judgment. I was diligently looking for his wild drive when I happened to stumble on a brand-new 'Dunlop'.

'What are you playing with?' I asked.

'Let me see,' he said, watching my face very intently' 'was it a "Colonel", or a "Zodiac", or a "Silver King", or – oh, I know; it was a 'Challenger".'

I put the ball in my pocket.

At the fourteenth, where Clerkson had the honour, some workmen were walking across the fairway, quite three hundred yards ahead.

'Do you think I can reach them?' my opponent asked. I thoughtlessly said, 'No, of course not'.

Directly he had driven he yelled 'Fore!' at the top of his voice. The men looked round.

'That was a narrow escape,' he gasped.

'But surely you were a long way short,' I said.

'Short!' he exclaimed, 'why, man, it was *right over their heads!*'

He gave me a rare fright at the next.

I had a splendid tee shot, for once, and Clerkson walked straight up to my ball.

'This is mine, I believe,' he said.

'Certainly not,' I cried, 'I am playing with a "Kite".'

"*So am I!*" said he.

Fortunately I was able to point out a private mark which I had made on my ball.

We were all square at the eighteenth. I drove out of bounds.

'Did you get a good one?' I asked anxiously, after he had played.

'A perfect peach,' he replied.

I concluded that I had lost the match. I persevered, however, and was playing two more with my approach, while he (so I was informed) was less than a yard from the hole. My mashie shot looked like going in, but the ball came to rest on the edge of the tin.

Clerkson walked up, looked at the ball, went on one knee, then suddenly dashed his cap on the ground in disgust.

'Anything wrong?' I inquired.

'Wrong?' he repeated. 'Can't you see that you have laid me *a dead stymie?*'

He studied the line with great care.

'I think there is just room to pull round,' he muttered.

He played, and watched, with an agonised expression, the course of his invisible ball.

Suddenly there came a strong puff of wind, and my ball toppled into the hole.

'D——n it all,' cried Clerkson, '*I've knocked you in!*'

He picked up my ball, and with it, apparently, his own.

'A halved match,' he said, 'and I must thank you for an exceedingly interesting game.'

I was due in London that evening, and on my return, some weeks later, I learnt that Clerkson had been laid up with a form of brain fever.

8

RETIRED GOLF

by Harry Graham

Harry graham's character Reginald Drake Biffin was a favourite with many readers between the two World Wars, and the volumes of stories about him are still widely appreciated and collected today. Biffin was famous as a chap who 'knew something about everything and everything about something' – and in one of the volumes (*The Complete Sportsman*) indeed held forth on everything from cricket to golf. Though Harry Graham never described himself as anything other than a very indifferent golfer, he had this to say of Biffin: 'On all matters connected with sport, Biffin proved himself over and over again to be an authority whose opinions were unquestioned, and whose experience was unrivalled.'

Biffin is certainly a man of ideas where improving the lot of the older golfer is concerned, as the reader will discover in 'Retired Golf' which was first published in 1919. I find it impossible not to laugh at him and with him!

RETIRED GOLF

I

It has been roughly estimated by competent statisticians that within comparatively recent times the game of golf has increased the cost of the State pension list by an annual sum of not less than £200,000. Before the Scottish national pastime had attained its present almost universal popularity, it was the fashion for superannuated officials who were past their work to betake themselves to cheerless villas in the neighbourhood of Camberley or Canterbury, where they strove to mitigate the tedium of a miserable existence of enforced leisure by writing violent letters to the newspapers to complain of the decadence of their native land.

Veteran Civil Servants spent the evenings of their lives giving the dog a run in a suburban lane, or tricycling to the

local post-office to inquire if there were any letters for Pon-
dicherry Lodge or The Chestnuts. Retired Major-Generals
were compelled to simulate a fictitious interest in intensive
gardening or philately; grey-headed Rear-Admirals of the
Blue wasted upon their wives or domestics that wealth of
cosmopolitan invective which they had laboriously acquired
in various parts of the world in the course of a hectic and
successful naval career. Imprecations that had sent a shudder
of apprehension rippling from stem to stern of a British
battleship spent themselves harmlessly upon the hardened
ears of devoted help-meet or female retainer; the rich beauty
of a lurid vocabulary that had been the envy of many a
quarter-deck was lost upon the jobbing gardener, while objur-
gations that had driven able-bodied seamen to cling in terror
to the aft hatchways left the boot-boy comparatively cold.

Thus, thwarted at every turn, hemmed in by the narrow
boundaries of parochial life, with no outlet for his energies, no
safety-valve for those eccentricities of temper that he had
cultivated so assiduously in every corner of the globe, the
retired official became a prey to those morbid self-analytical
thoughts which, fostered by periodical attacks of gout, and
liberally stimulated with doses of rare old tawny port at two
shillings the bottle, led often enough to a premature and
untimely decease. Major-Generals perished of suppressed
passion before they had reached seventy; Admirals exploded
at an even earlier age; Indian Civil Servants acquired the fatal
bath-chair habit while still in their prime; and few pensioners
survived for any length of time to enjoy the £200 or so a year
with which a grateful country rewards those who have
devoted the best part of their life to its service.

This sad state of affairs has been mercifully put to an end by
the discovery of a game which not only prolongs the span of
human existence and reduces the ranks of the chronically
moribund, but also invests the lives of the aged with an interest that unquestionably enhances their domestic happiness,
and renders many of them quite tolerable husbands and
fathers.

The victim of advancing years, of senile decay, of incipient
dotage, may find in golf a panacea for, a palliative of, almost

every mental and physical disability under which he happens to labour; the martyr to that nervous irritability which too often accompanies second childhood is supplied with a fresh channel for the expression of those thoughts which, if unhealthily restrained, cast their shadow over home-life and bring discord into the family circle.

I knew a retired Army Colonel who at one time used to make his wife's existence a positive burden to her by abusing the cooking; who habitually sat at meals in a gloomy silence that was only broken by the sound of his plate being pushed away from him with a snort of disgust. To-day, since he has taken to golf, this man is an altered being, displaying a healthy appetite for whatever food is placed before him, and talking happily away all through dinner upon the subject in which he is now absorbingly interested. Often, indeed, his flow of genial garrulity continues until long after bedtime; he will keep his wife awake half the night describing the three perfect putts he made upon the last green; he will rouse her at 2 a.m. to tell her of a mashie shot which he had forgotten to mention at dinner, and far into the dawn his voice can be heard explaining to a snoring and unconscious spouse that he would most assuredly have done the fourth hole in six if only he hadn't missed his drive, required three strokes to get out of a bunker, and taken four more to hole out.

Again, a Rear-Admiral of my acquaintance, the violence of whose language had long rendered him an insupportable inmate of any respectable household, became a reformed character once he had learnt to play golf. After spending a strenuous day hacking his ball from tussock to tussock in the 'rough' at Walton Heath, he would return home so hoarse and exhausted as to be unable to utter a single word of reproof to his family. In the Navy he had been justly considered unique as a master of invective, but on the golf-links he often became inspired by adverse fortune to surpass even his own earlier efforts, and the heights of eloquence to which he soared, the maledictory phrases which he spontaneously coined in his attempts to do justice to his outraged feelings, earned the admiration of local Masters of Hounds, and would have wrung reluctant tributes from the most imaginative fish-porters in Billingsgate.

II

It is not my purpose in these pages to deal with the technicalities of golf, nor yet to emulate the literary labours of such expert essayists as Braid, Vardon, or Taylor. Of what is known as 'Advanced Golf' these writers have treated in a manner which less competent masters of English prose may well have cause to envy; they have covered the whole ground so completely that nothing remains to be said upon this particular aspect of the game.

Very little, however, has yet been written upon the subject of what (for lack of a better term) I may venture to call 'Retired Golf' – that is to say, golf for the elderly, for players whose handicap ranges between 18 and 36, who may truthfully be said to have one foot in the grave and the other almost continually in some bunker. And it is to these, as well as to the mentally deficient, the morally and physically infirm, and to all natural and incurable foozlers, that I propose to address a few words of counsel and encouragement, in the hope that by so doing I may possibly help to improve their game, and thus add not a little to the sum of human happiness.

The whole secret of success at retired golf, as everybody nowadays admits, lies in the ability of the player to strike the ball *without moving his head*. The constantly repeated injunction to 'keep your eye on the ball' is, indeed, very often misleading, this optical immobility being only enjoined as the most practical method of ensuring that the head shall be kept perfectly still.

Few men, alas! are privileged to possess swivel-eyes, and for those fortunate beings who are thus naturally equipped with the advantages usually monopolized by chameleons it is easy to remove the gaze without shifting the head. But with the majority of mankind the eye cannot be raised with impunity, the temptation to lift up their heads – after the fashion of the Psalmist's everlasting gates – at the moment of hitting the ball being almost irresistible. Many systems have therefore been invented by golfers anxious to break themselves of this pernicious habit, but it will be sufficient for my purpose if I describe the two most successful now in vogue at St. Andrews.

The first (and perhaps the simplest) consists of wearing a tall hat in which a number of small sleigh-bells have been carefully concealed. It then becomes the player's chief ambition to strike his ball without ringing the bells, and whenever he succeeds in so doing he may be quite sure that, whatever other fault he may have committed, he has not moved his head. That occasionally, even in such circumstances, his strike falls short of perfection may be accounted for by the fact that he has pulled his arms in, pushed his elbows out, shifted his feet, altered his stance, lost his balance, or been guilty of one or other of the thousand minor crimes with which the path of the golfer is ever beset.

The top-hat method, however, possesses certain inevitable drawbacks, some of which are so patent as scarcely to require mention. I remember once at Sandwich, when I happened to be wearing the sleighbell form of headgear, and was strolling along the fairway in a very musical fashion, a parlourmaid came running out of an adjacent villa, under the impression that I was the local muffin-man, and, pressing sixpence into my unwilling palm, besought me to supply her with half a dozen of my choicest crumpets for her mistress's afternoon tea. Not happening on this particular afternoon to have any crumpets about me, my confusion may well be imagined.

On another occasion, at Brancaster, I was followed for miles along the 'pretty' by some two hundred bleating sheep, who had mistaken me for the bell-wether of the flock; and when a couple of short-horn cattle joined the procession, the congestion upon the putting-greens became so great that, at my opponent's urgent request, I consented to doff the offending hat, and bury the sleigh-bells in a bunker.

A much simpler way of keeping the head immovable consists of tying a stout string to a tooth in the lower jaw, passing the end through one's legs, and getting a caddy to hold it tightly behind one's back while one is addressing the ball. In this case any attempt to jerk the head up results in the loss of a favourite molar, and it is safe to assume that a man of even moderate intelligence will gladly renounce the most seductive of bad habits before excessive indulgence therein has left him completely toothless. To prove the efficacy of this system I have but to mention that in the summer of 1907 I succeeded in reducing my handicap from 32 to 28 at the negligible cost of two wisdom teeth. Need I say more?

I cannot honestly recommend the practice in vogue among some of the older habitués of our Lowland golf-courses who paint a large human eye upon their golf-ball, and have it teed up in such a way that it glares upon the player with a passionate intensity which makes it almost impossible for him to look away.

This may be satisfactory enough on the tee, unfortunately, the painted eye will not always remain uppermost when once the ball is in play, and it becomes a difficult matter to negotiate a successful approach shot with a ball that is either gazing invitingly into an impending hazard or seems to be winking sardonically at one from the 'rough'.

The late Lord Chorlesbury always used a ball of this kind, and I shall never forget the panic that ensued among the nurses and children who spend their days on the beach to the right of the third tee at North Berwick when what appeared to be a gigantic human (or, as some of them thought, Divine) eye fell in their midst from the blue vault of Heaven above.

Two French governesses, professed atheists, who happened to be bathing in the sea, and were at the same time engaged in a theological discussion in which they ridiculed the alleged immanence of a Supreme Being, were converted then and there to a mild form of agnosticism, and reluctantly admitted the plausibility of that uncomfortable doctrine which presupposes the perpetual presence of a Divine Power 'about one's bath, and about one's bed, and spying out all one's ways'.

In spite of this system, however, Lord Chorlesbury was probably the most erratic driver in the world. He is the only man I have ever met who could strike his ball so far back on the heel of his club that it would speed through his legs at right angles from the tee, and injure an inoffensive caddy standing behind him. To play as his partner or opponent was to take one's life in one's hand; and it was with especial reference to his peculiar method that the Bishop of Deal composed that well-known hymn 'For those in Peril on the Tee', which has since become so popular with mixed foursomes on every seaside course in Christendom.

III

Once the player has learnt to control the movements of his head he may be said to have mastered the game of golf, and can confidently set forth to give an exhibition of his prowess upon the most crowded links without any very serious internal misgivings. There are, however, one or two minor points of golfing etiquette with which it is as well that he should be acquainted if he desires to be regarded as an attractive partner or a tolerable opponent.

When two second-class players start out together from the club-house to enjoy a friendly match, it is always considered proper for each of them to deprecate his own skill, and express modest doubts as to his ability to provide his companion with a good game.

'I don't feel as if I should be able to hit the ball at all,' he murmurs diffidently. 'I haven't played for weeks.'

'Nor I,' replies his friend. 'I expect you'll beat me hollow. I've got a groggy elbow, too.'

'I'm sorry to hear that,' says the first. 'To tell you the truth, I'm not feeling very fit myself. We sat up playing bridge last night till any hour, and . . .'

'I never sleep well in this place; I don't know why it is, I'm sure. And with my groggy elbow . . .'

'You ought to give me a strike a hole, at least . . .'

'My dear chap! What's your handicap?'

'I don't believe I've got one. I play so little. What's yours?'

'Mine? Oh, mine's anything between eighteen and twenty. And then with my groggy elbow . . .'

'How do you and Jones play together?'

'Oh, he beats me easily. At least, last time we played he gave me a half and won, six up; but then I must admit I had the most infernal luck and got into every single bunker on the course. I began right enough; did the first hole in nine, the second in eleven, and the third in eight. After that I seemed to go all to pieces.'

'Suppose we play even?'

'Righto! After all, so long as we have a decent game, it doesn't matter much who wins.'

And at golf, fortunately, a decent game can always be obtained. It is, indeed, one of the chief charms of this attractive pastime that, by means of a system of tactful handicapping, players of every degree and class may be evenly matched against one another in a fashion that can seldom be accomplished at other games. A single bad lawn-tennis player will ruin a whole set; at croquet or billiards the man who is matched against a champion spends most of his time idly watching his opponent playing, and only issues at rare intervals from a retirement into which he is almost immediately driven back. At golf, on the other hand, the receipt of a few strokes enables an indifferent performer to hold his own against a superior adversary, and there are other methods by which golfers of varying skill can be placed upon an equal footing.

It is, of course, notorious that the player who is permitted under the terms of his handicap to shout 'Boo!' in the ear of an opponent three times in the course of a round, just as the unfortunate man is addressing his ball, possesses an advantage which should always enable him to secure the match. The right to 'Boo!' need never, as a matter of fact, be exercised, the mere knowledge that this exclamation is perpetually dangling like the sword of Damocles over his head being as a rule quite sufficient to put the most experienced player off his game. With eighteen bisques and a couple of 'Boos!' I should be quite ready to challenge Vardon himself.

IV

Golf has frequently been labelled a selfish game by persons who do not indulge in the sport; nevertheless, it may be justly affirmed that scarcely a round passes without providing opportunities for a display of generosity, patience, and other kindred virtues, of which unselfishness is the very essence.

It is, for instance, an essential characteristic of the true golfer that he should be able to praise an opponent's good strokes and sympathise with his bad ones in a natural and whole-hearted fashion, and at the shortest possible notice. When he is four down at the turn, and his adversary lays his second shot dead, or when his rival's drive drops like a stone into a bunker, it is no easy task to exclaim 'Well played!' or 'Bad luck!' (as the case may be) in tones that carry conviction. 'In thinking of the sorrows of others,' as a great philosopher once remarked, 'we forget our own,' and the truth of this saying is nowhere more apparent than upon the golf-links.

The perfect golfer should always be ready to listen with a kindly ear to all the reasons his opponent insists upon giving him for missing various easy shots; he should at the same time remember that nobody really cares for unsolicited information of this kind, and should refrain from remarking, after he has foozled a particularly easy mashie-shot: 'My ball was lying in a hole!' 'I looked up!' or 'My caddy gave me the wrong club!'

Long experience upon the links teaches one to be genially tolerant of the mathematical miscalculations of others. It is a strange thing that men who invariably add up a bridge score correctly – City magnates, captains of industry, masters of finance who can tell offhand the profit they have made on 460 Canadian Pacific ordinary shares when the stock rises $3\frac{5}{8}$ – often display a lamentable incapacity for estimating the exact number of times they have struck a golf-ball between the tee and the green.

Persons of unblemished reputation and scrupulous integrity will entirely forget whether they took three or four strokes to get out of a bunker; the fact that their first drive went out of bounds, and that they were forced to play a second shot from the tee, escapes their memory in a way that non-golfers might deem incredible. It therefore often becomes a task of uncommon delicacy to remind an adversary of strokes that have apparently made no sort of impression upon his memory, without seeming to cast aspersions upon his honesty of purpose. And when, on the other hand, he adduces conclusive evidence to prove that one has taken eight shots to reach the hole, after one has confidently declared oneself to be 'dead' in five, it is difficult not to temper one's apologies with resentment.

The art of winning or losing gracefully at any game is never a very easy one to acquire, and at golf it is only a whit less objectionable to evince signs of unconcealed elation at being 'five up' than it is to stride along with a pale face and set jaw, declining to utter a civil word in reply to one's opponent's sympathetic comments, just because one happens to be 'five down'.

My cousin, Colonel Waters, was one of those players with whom it was impossible to play unless he chanced to be winning. The look of concentrated loathing which he cast upon a more fortunate rival was enough to spoil the pleasure of any game, and as soon as he became 'two down', he would adopt an attitude of mute melancholia that rendered him the least desirable golfing companion in the world. At Hoylake, indeed, Colonel Waters was very generally known as 'Siloam' – he had, they flippantly said, such a troubled face!

In one respect alone is it fair to say that golf is a selfish pastime; it is perhaps the only game that a man can pleasurably and profitably play *all by himself*.

An attempt to play lawn-tennis all alone is seldom satisfactory; indeed, my uncle, Horace Biffin, is one of the few men I ever heard of who seems to have derived any amusement from this form of entertainment. Even so the result was often more interesting for spectators than for the single player. You see, Uncle Horace was compelled by the exigencies of the situation to lob his service very high into the air, in order that he might be able to run round to the other side of the net in time to return the ball; and he never dared to send it back with any violence if he wished to sprint round again in time to take his return. At the back of his mind, therefore, there lay the perpetual consciousness that he could always defeat himself if he desired, and this deprived the game of much of its interest, and robbed the player of a good deal of his natural zest. Uncle Horace, indeed, would often become so tired of rushing wildly round to the opposite court to take his own services that he was tempted now and then to serve eight consecutive faults into the net, so as to bring the set to an end; and it is not to be wondered at that long before he had reached the age of eighty, he should have decided to renounce lawn-tennis in favour of golf.

At the latter game, as I have already remarked, a solitary player can enjoy a sufficiently exciting game either by matching himself with Bogey or by playing two balls, one against the other, from the tee. Colonel Waters, to whose eccentricities of conduct I have alluded above, when he began to find it increasingly difficult to persuade anybody to play with him, adopted the latter system, to his own and everybody's extreme satisfaction.

He would start out in the morning with two caddies, two sets of clubs, and two balls – a 'Silver King' and a 'Colonel' – and engage in the most thrilling contests against himself, from which he invariably emerged victorious. In these games he had no chance of displaying those peculiarities of temper which rendered him so unpopular among his fellows, for his rage at being laid a stymie by himself was mitigated by his feelings of joy at having laid himself a stymie; and whenever his 'Silver King' rolled into a bunker, he found comfort in the fact that his 'Colonel' was lying safely on the 'pretty' or *vice versa*. Furthermore, he was enabled to invest the game with a spice of inexpensive adventure by laying a small shade of odds against either ball, and at the end of the day he could extract a morbid pleasure from writing himself a cheque for the amount he had won and lost, and sending it to the bank upon which it was drawn, to be placed to the credit of his account. Would that all gambling transactions – as the dear Dowager Bishop of Monte Carlo once said to me – would that all gambling transactions could be conducted so innocently, with so inconsiderable a loss of treasure and of *amour-propre!*

V

Among advanced Socialists and other persons who entertain exaggerated views upon the Dignity of Labour, the use of a caddy to carry clubs and construct tees is regarded as a grave blemish upon an otherwise harmless pursuit. With equal justice might one resent the employment of a groundman to roll the pitch after each innings at cricket, or consider that the presence of a professional marker detracted from the merits of billiards.

The first-class caddy is in no sense of the phrase a beast of burden; for the time being he becomes the sympathetic confidant, often the autocratic adviser, of a man who is probably his superior socially, intellectually, and financially. Indeed, the friendly intercourse between player and caddy paves the way for that better feeling between class and class which in these latter democratic days affords so hopeful a sign of social regeneration.

As I write these words I cannot help recalling a touching scene that indelibly impressed itself upon my mental retina, and to a great extent bears out the truth of my contention. It was on the links at Lossiemouth, last summer, where one of the greatest living British statesmen was anxiously inspecting his ball as it lay in the rough about thirty yards to the right of the eleventh hole. Uncertain as to which club to select for so important an approach shot, he turned for counsel to his caddy, a small Scottish lad of some ten summers. The pair formed one of the prettiest pictures imaginable: on the one hand the grey-headed but perplexed statesman, gravely urging the advisability of taking a mashie; on the other the ragged, bare-footed tousle-headed urchin, insisting upon the use of a niblick. From the serious expression upon the eminent politician's face he might well have been consulting a Cabinet colleague upon some question of vital import to the Empire, and I watched with interest to see the upshot of their deliberations.

It was all in vain that the hard-headed Minister of State, the man in whose hands lay the destinies of a great people, pleaded for his mashie; the bare-footed urchin stubbornly shook his head, and with an imperious gesture thrust the niblick into his employer's hand. Shrugging his shoulders in that resigned fashion that the House of Commons knows so well, the statesman took the proffered club, and in another moment had laid his ball within six inches of the hole. Do you wonder, dear reader, that as I turned away from this moving scene, with a lump in my throat and the tears starting to my eyes, I should have felt that I had at last learnt something of the qualities that render constitutional party government possible – that I had discovered, perhaps, some inkling of what it is that makes us Britons what we are? Yes – or, rather, no.

VI

There comes a day, alas! in the lives of all of us when, under the stress of advancing years, the field-sports in which we were wont to indulge lose much of their pristine charm. The ping-pong racket is relegated to the lumber-chest, the skates hang rusting in the pantry cupboard, the beribboned oar is sent with the discarded cricket-bat to swell the Vicar's jumble sale, the croquet-mallet languishes among the grandchildren's perambulators in the telephone-room.

But though the niblick becomes a burden and the desire to drive a long ball from the tee fails, the golfer need not give way to utter despair. Even in his dotage he may still hope to extract a not altogether exiguous pleasure from striking a captive ball into a net in the back-garden, and can find endless satisfaction in the task of converting the lawn-tennis court into a putting-green for 'clock-golf'. And when at last he is no longer able to leave the house, he can amuse himself by laying out a miniature golf-links in his wife's drawing-room, and dodder round with a couple of clubs, seeking to establish a record for the course.

In 'house-golf' (as it is called) the various articles of domestic furniture will usually supply all the hazards required, though these may be further supplemented, if necessary, by obstacles imported from outside. Thus, a hip-bath filled with the moss-fibre in which last year's bulbs were grown makes an excellent bunker; two waste-paper baskets piled upon a low book-case add to the difficulties of a mashie-shot from the sofa on to the hearth-rug, where an inverted saucer adequately fulfils the purpose of a hole.

In the drawing-rooms of most of the Stately Homes of England little courses of this kind have been planned by loving hands, and the aristocratic inmates are thus provided with a source of innocent occupation that the most selfish Socialist could scarcely grudge them.

It is true that old Lady Chorlesbury used to point with horror to the holes made by her husband's niblick in the best Wilton carpet, and found but little comfort in his solemn promise to replace the divots, she nevertheless realised that it would be cruel to deprive the old gentleman of such a means of solace in his declining years, and at Chorlesbury House 'drawing-room golf' was always winked at, if not actively encouraged.

I happened to be having tea there one evening last winter when Lord Chorlesbury tottered in on the arm of his valet, and challenged me to a friendly game. To humour him I consented to play, though I had no nails in my boots, and was forced to borrow the butler's clubs.

On his own home links, I need hardly say, I was no match for my host, his knowledge of the course giving him a decided advantage, as was soon only too apparent. At the very first hole – a dog-leg hole round a lacquer screen, with a china-cupboard guarding the green – after being stymied by a bust of the late Dr Livingstone and having on two occasions to lift my ball without penalty from casual ink on the writing-table, I lost my nerve. And when, at the second, I found myself in a hopeless lie behind a marble clock on the mantelpiece, I picked up in despair. I shall never forget his lordship's delight, later on in the game, on his becoming 'Dormy two', when a pretty approach shot of mine was caught by the keyboard of the piano, and I hooked my next into the coal-scuttle (taking three to get out), while with a fine lofting shot over an occasional-table my host laid his ball dead on the hearth-rug in four.

Lady Chorlesbury watched the game with interest from a chair near the window, and it was tacitly agreed (in accordance with a local by-law) that whenever a ball struck her on the head and bounded off into the rough, the player should be allowed to have the strike over again; while if it remained in her lap, she should be regarded as 'ground under repair', and the ball be lifted without a penalty.

Lord Chorlesbury was indeed a true sportsman; to the very end of his life he helped to keep alive that spirit of sport upon which our Imperial greatness so largely depends. One of his last acts was to despatch a postal order for five shillings to the Olympic Talent Fund when it seemed possible that the subscriptions might fall short by some £90,000 of the desired total. At his lamented demise, *Golf Illustrated* published a lifelike portrait of him, which I have cut out and hung in the spare bedroom; and when I am slicing badly, or have temporarily lost the art of 'putting', I go and gaze at this picture of the man who provided the world with a perfect example of all that a Retired Golfer should be, whose handicap was never less than 30, but who never gave up hope. Peace to his mashies!

9

JAN PLAYS GOLF

by A. J. Coles

JAN STEWER was another very popular humorous character who appeared in a series of books between the two World Wars. He lived in a small Devon village and possessed an insatiable curiosity about people and the world in general. His adventures were related in the dialect of that lovely part of the country and the stories contained in books such as *A Parcel of Ol' Crams, In Chimley Corner* and *Yap* found a large and appreciative audience throughout the whole of the country.

Author A. J. Coles was a Devon man by birth and so thoroughly integrated himself into the character of Jan Stewer that, rather like Sir Arthur Conan Doyle with Sherlock Holmes, the creation came to overshadow the creator. The story which follows, 'Jan Plays Golf', is as uproariously funny as anything A. J. Coles wrote about the droll old Devonian – and in its portrait of a man who imagines *anyone* can play golf, he cleverly mirrors an attitude that a great many other people have also shared – until, that is, they have actually *tried* the game for themselves. . .

JAN PLAYS GOLF

1. SEEING HOW IT IS DONE

They tell me zome people takes years to larn the way to play golf. All I can zay is, I thought I was middlin' thick-'aided, but I'm jiggered if it took me years, ner yet months. Not even wiks. Two days is all I had; wan day watchin' others at it, and wan day others watchin' me. And that's how long it took me to pick up all I knaws about golf and all I wants to knaw. Two days; and I've larned sufficient to last me a lifetime.

Tommy Bamfield was the wan what beguiled me into it. I

alwis use to look upon Tommy as a friend o' mine, but I shan't never trust'n no more. I shan't never trust nobody what gives their mind to golf, 'cus 'tis the most desatefullest, diddlin' paacel of jiggery-pokery that was ever invented.

I'll tell 'ee all about it.

Mr Bamfield is the ocshineer auver to Barleycombe. He's properly mazed about this-yer golf caper, and he was everlastin' keepin' on to me to go with 'n and try me hand to it. I kep' saying p'r'aps I wude when I had the time to spare, so wan day he said:

'Jan,' he says, 'I be comin' to call for you nex' Zaturdy in my moter to take 'ee to the golf.'

'So do,' I said. I wad'n so very anxious about the golf part, but I thought if he mind to take me fer a nice ride, us wude'n vall out about that.

When I went 'ome and told my Ann about it her was most mortle excited.

'You'll be auver there amongs' all the better-most volk to Barleycombe,' her said. ''Tis something fer Mr Bamfield to pick on you like that. He've never took no other body from Muddlecombe village to the golf bevore, seps Dr Jinkins and Squire Porter. They'm the only two in this parish what goes to the golf, so you ought to think yerzel' 'ighly 'onnered.'

Ees, and durin' the nex' vew days I'm beggered if her did'n manage to let every other wumman in the village have the news. Did'n matter what subjic' they was on upon, her'd scheme it around zome-'ow to fit it in that her ole man was gwain off with the gen'lvolks to Barleycombe to take part in the golf.

O' coorse, her had'n got no more idaya what it was to do than what I had. All her trouble was, what clothes I ought to wear.

'You daun't want to go there looking' like a gawk,' her says, 'and let 'em think you dunnaw all about it.'

'I daun't zee why I shude want to stap 'em from thinkin' the truth,' I says. 'I daun't know the fust thing about it, never mind *all* about it.'

But that did'n satisfy mother. Her reckoned I had'n got nuff self-pride.

'There's sure to be proper clothes to wear for the purpose,' her says, 'same's there is with cricket and vootbaal. I'd sooner you spend a vew shullin's and went auver there lookin' proper vitty than to go shawin' yer ignerance and makin' a table-talk. I'll ax Mr Annaferd. He reads the paapers a lot, and very likely he cude tell a body.'

So nex' time her zee'd Ned go past the houze her called 'n een and putt the matter to 'en.

'Well, missis,' sayd Ned, 'I dunnaw that I can tell 'ee very much, but from what I can make out, they gener'ly wears what they calls plush-vowers.'

'That's right,' says Ann. 'Now you come to mention it, I've yer'd 'em tell about they plush-vowers. What be 'um like, Mr Annaferd?'

'That I can't tell 'ee, missis.'

'I wonder where I cude vind out,' her says. 'I've got they ole plush curtins upstairs which us never uses. There's vower o' thay, so 'twude be jis' right. If I cude get the pattern I dersay I cude run 'em up with the machine.'

'No, you waun't do nothin' o' the sort,' I says. 'If you thinks I be gwain auver there trigged out in plush curtins you'd better think again, and think zummat difer'nt.'

'Daun' be so stoobid,' says mother. 'Who's gwain to know they was curtins? They'm the very best plush that money can buy. They'm hardly faded a bit, and see the years they hanged up to the winders.'

'Well, you can hang 'em up there again,' I says. 'You ban't gwain to hang 'em on me, so I tell 'ee straight.'

But mother cude'n let it rest, and bothered if her did'n go right away up to Tilda Grinnaway, the dressmaker, to zee if her cude tell her aught about plush-vowers. Tilda went rummagin' amongs' a heap o' they fashin bukes and furridged out wan with a picsher of a chap in this-yer rig-out. Vine job that was, and mother come rinning home with 'n, to show me what I ought to look like. You never zee'd sitch a sight in your life. 'Twas nothin' more ner less than a gash'ly-lookin pair o' burches about ten sizes too big. They looked fer all the gude in the world like a couple o' rag-bags with holes in the bottom vor the veet to poke out.

'I cude make a pair like that,' her says.

'Yas, and you can wear 'em, too,' I says. 'I daun' doubt fer wan minute but what you cude make 'em. But not vor me.'

'Daun' be so sauft. I want to send 'ee auver there dressed proper.'

'That's right, mother. But if I was to wear they things I shude consider I was dressed improper. So daun' 'ee zay no more about it. There's gwain to be no plush-vowers vor me. I'll wait till I be zick and tired o' life and then I'll have a pair of plush-eights and go out and drown mezelf in 'em.'

So I weared the same togs as what I wude if I was gwain into Ex'ter, and when I got to the plaace I found I wad'n no differ'nt to the rest. I did zee a couple o' chaps with they rag-bags on, but they wad'n plush. Only ordnery cloth.

Mr Bamfield come to call fer me with his moter, same's he said he wude, and drived me to the golf plaace. I'd bin thinkin' matters auver, and I'd made up me mind I wude'n take no part in it, fust go off, but only watch the rest and get a bit of idaya what 'twas like. Then I shude'n be so likely to make a fule o' mezell when it come to my turn. I told Tommy that, gwain in-along. I thought p'r'aps he'd be a bit upzot, but he wad'n.

'If you think you'd rather do that, Jan,' he says, ''twill suit me better. Matter o' fact,' he says, 'I met with a gen'lman 's-mornin' from up-the-country who's suppaused to take a middlin' gude hand to it, and as I be considered wan o' the best in our club, he beggid o' me to give'n a game, and 'tis the only chance us have got. But I cude aisy vind zomebody to have a round with you, so's you shan't be disappointed.'

'No disappointing about it, Mr Bamfield. I'd sooner look on at you two, if you daun' objec'.'

'I dunnaw but what 'twude'n be all-so-well, Jan,' he says. 'You'd be able to get zome idaya o' the game bevore you venter on it.'

So that's what I done, and I got idaya o' the game all right. But 'twad'n hardly the idaya he reckoned I was gwain to get.

I'll explain in a minute what they two fellers done, and then you shall tell me if 'twad'n more like a couple o' skule chillern itemmin' about than two middle-age men.

Fust of all us went in what they calls the club-'ouze. That's a vine swell plaace with butiful aisy cheers sticked about. I wondered to zee so many aisy cheers till I'd vinished me day's golf, and then I vound the raison vor 'em. I'm darned if a feller can't do with a aisy cheer arter wan gude go at that caper. I shude be vor taking wan along with me.

I alwis thought they played in a vield. Laur bless yer zaul, they can't do with a vield; they wants a distric'. Wance you've started out, you'm zummin like the chap what went seekin' fer the North Pole; you never knaws when you'll be comin' back again.

My dear days, it only shows what amount o' trouble and bother zome volks will go to so long as you don't call it work. If they two fellers had bin made to trapes all they miles and go droo such a paasel of manoovers just to plaise zome other body, what a fuss they wude 'a-made. They'd have played Amlick, I'll warran' they wude. If they was forced to do it in the ordnery way o' business they'd consider they was the hardest done by of any volks on the face o' the earth.

The other gen'lman was there waitin' in the club'-ouze, and very nice he was, too, before he started on with the golf, and then I'm jiggered if he wad'n a proper nuisance. Well, they'm all the zame, come to that. They waun' spaik a word about nothin' else. You can't yer nothin' but 'andy-caps, and foozlums, and bunkums, and mashers and bibble-its, and putts and chips, and how many strokes they can make to the hour or the mile, I ban't sure which. If you mentions anybody's name to try and change the subjic', all they can zay is, 'What's his 'andy-cap?'

And their tays. They keeped on tellin' about tay, and I tell 'ee straight I cude 'a-done with a dish o' tay very well. But it all ended with talk. I did'n zee no sign o' tay, ner nothin' else. I'd 'a-gived a shullin and welcome vor a pint o' zider. Bevore us had gone half the journey I cude'n spit a zixpence. Yet every now and again they'd bring up about the tay, which only made it wiss.

And then, whatever do you think they come to talkin' about next? When they cude'n think o' nort else nonsensical they start tellin' about bogies. Bogies, mind 'ee! Two grawed up men yappin' about bogies. If it had a-bin pixies it wude'n

[90]

'a-bin so bad. But when they started on about bogies I thought
to mezell, 'It only shows 'ee what a state o' mind golf can bring
anybody to.'

But laur, what else can you expec' when you come to
witness the game? When us was in readiness to start they
tooked a bagful o' sticks apiece and marched off.

Us stopped when us come to a bit of a flat plaace and they
both chucked their bags down on the ground. But each aw'm
tooked out wan stick with a nob on the end. And that's when
they started makin' sillies o' theirzel's.

Fust of all the gen'lman went to a li'l box and tooked out a
han'ful o' durt. And what do you suppause he done wai' 't? He
stoopied down and made a li'l heap on the ground. I thought
he was tryin' to be funny jis' to make us laaf, but I zee'd
Tommy Bamfield wad'n gwain to laaf, so I took it to be that
the poor feller was a bit tiched up under the roof, as the sayin'
is. Natcherly, I veeled sorry vor 'en. But when he fished out a
li'l white ball and sticked he up on tap o' the heap o' durt, I
thought I shude 'a-bust out.

And then if you'd zee'd the antics he went droo arter that,
I'll make a bet you'd 'a-roared. He went and stood bezide
this-yer ball with the stick in his hand, spraid out his veet and
started aimin' at the ball with the nob on the end o' the stick.
About a dizzen times he aimed at 'n, as if he was promisin'
what he'd do to 'en if he did'n behave hiszell. Then he stopped
and lookid all around to zee if anybody was watchin' aw 'n.
And I daun' wonder at it, nuther. He wude'n wish fer any
stranger to zee 'en make sitch a fule of hiszell, for certin. Then
he aimed to the ball again a time or two and I thought to
mezell, 'Now he's gwain to knack 'n.'

But no. He stapped back away from the ball and started
siwshin' his stick around, knackin' off bits o' grass. Then he
come back to the ball again and lookid at 'n, as gude as to zay,
'How fer gudeness sake did you get there?'

Then he started itchin' his veet as if he was squaishin' a
black-biddle. Next he beginned to wriggle his body, like a
chap with a flay in the middle of his back where he can't
scratch 'n. Then all-to-once, he up with his stick and he
fetched thik poor li'l ball sitch a clout, and hat 'n so-fur as he

cude zee 'en. Wonder to me he did'n knack the inzide right out aw'n.

'Caw!' I thought to mezell, 'that's the the end o' that wan, for certin. Do he get a cigar for that, I wonder, or a nit?'

Well, and then I'm blawed if Tommy did'n go droo precisely the zame antics, and he hat a ball likewise. Then they both picked up their bags and walked off.

'Have us got to go and vind they balls?' I said.

'Certin'ly,' says Tommy. 'What do 'ee think?'

'I think,' I says, 'that if you did'n whack 'em hardly so hard us wude vind 'em a lot more aisy.'

However, us found 'em all right, and then I'm jiggered if they did'n take another stick apiece, and fetch they balls another whack. Then us had to trapes arter 'em again. Well, I was beginnin' to get a bit weary of walkin' about lookin' fer balls, so I said:

'How many times do you reckon you'm gwain to do this bevore you begins to play?'

Then I found they was playin', if you plaise. This was part of it.

Arter they'd give the balls another scat or two, us come to a nice flat bit 'o grass with a hole in the middle about the size of a quart pot, and they both trucked their balls into the hole.

'Is that the finish?' I said to Tommy.

'No, ti-no. That's the fust hole. Us goes on to the second, now.'

And then, by Jo, they went droo the zame ole pantomine again. Li'l heap o' durt, ball on the tap, the stick with the nob on the end, squashin' the black-biddle, flay down the middle o' the back, then, Whack! Away goes the balls. Away goes we to vind 'em. Bim-by us come to another li'l hole in the grass, and they truckled in their balls again. From what I can make out, 'tis the wan what can get his ball into the hole fust.

Two mortle howers us went on like that, scattin' the balls as fur as they'd go and then lookin' vor 'em. Us trapesed miles, and keeped on vindin' fresh li'l holes all auver the place. Zometimes wan o' they fellers wude scat his ball a bit ockerd and 'twude go off the track into the vuz or the brimmles. Then us might be there tain minutes or more seekin' vor 'n. You'd 'a-thought, sooner than waste all that time, they'd have a fresh ball. Bit if it had bin golden suvrins they cude'n be more keen to vind 'en. And what was the gude? When they *did* vind 'en they only whack 'n furder again.

And that's all 'twas, all the way droo the piece; whack, walk and look; whack, walk and look, and then dap it in a hole. You counts how many scats you gives 'en before he goes een, and the wan what gives the laistest number o' scats is the winner. I made out that much.

But I thought to mezell, 'You tell about larnin' to play golf! What is there to larn, fer gudeness saake? Nort. Any fule cude do this. I wish I had'n said I wude'n take part,' I said to mezell. 'I'll make a bet I cude scat thik ball furder than eether-wan o' they cude. I'll bet a guinea I cude.'

Bim-by, arter us had trapesed half-ways round the world, us got back to club-'ouze, and Tommy said, 'What be gwain to have, Jan?'

'Twas the fus' sainsible remark he'd made since us started.

Tom reckoned he'd winned the golf by wan hole, and he'd had zempty-nine scats to the ball. He zimmed to consider that was very gude, and zo did the tother gen'lman, but I thought 'twas a doost of a lot, mezell.

'Caw, darn my rigs,' I thought, 'if I cude'n hat thik ball around that distance in less knocks than zempty-nine I'd ait the li'l toad, stick and all.'

'Twas too laate fer me to have a go at it them, so I promised I'd go auver again the volleyin' Zaturdy and have a game 'long o' Mr Bamfield.

'I shall be yer waitin' vor 'ee, Jan,' he says. 'If you can manage to come auver on the bus, I'll drive 'ee home.'

2. SHOWING HOW TO DO IT

I'll take back all I've said about the blimmin' ole golf. I wish to gudeness I cude take back the whole blessid thing, so's nobody wude'n know nothin' about it. But 'tis too laate fer that. Wan o' these vine days I shall yer the last aw't, but 'twaun't be yet a bit, I'm 'fraid.

Where I made mistake to, I opened me mouthe a bit too

soon and a lot too wide. Like a gude many else, I used me tonge fust, instaid o' keepin' aw'n till last. What I ought to have done, if I'd had any sainse, I thought to have held me noise till I'd bin droo the whole rigmarole, and then zay whatever I'd got to zay. I shude have bin tellin' about what I knowed, instaid of what I thought I knowed, which is a very differ'nt thing. Instaid o' tellin' the volks what I'd done, I went tellin' 'em what I was gwain to do, and that's a fule's way o' gwain to work. Never say too much about what you'm gwain to do, speshly if 'tis zummat you've never done bevore. If you do, ten to wan you'll make yerzell a laafin'-sport, same as zomebody have done that I cude mention by name.

Natcherly, when I got back from the golf everybody wanted to know what I thought about it. And like a gawk I told 'em. ''Tis cheel's play,' I said, 'and you can't call it no other. Scattin' a li'l ball with a long stick and then gwain arter it, what else can you term that but cheel's play? And then they tells about larnin' to do it, as if there was aught to larn about it. If Tom Trott, there, was to let his li'l Jimmy have a walkin'-stick and a doornob, I cude larn 'en all there is to larn about golf in two minutes. They've got to get up to all manner o' redeclus antics, aimin', and measurin' and stiddin', and pre-parin' and luggin' about a gurt bag o' tools, jis' to pretend 'tis difficult, and make out they'm very clever. I'll make a bet I'd hat the ball furder than eether-wan aw'm, wai'out all thik ole pantomime.'

That's what I said, and a lot more bezides, becus if a chap ab'm got sainse nuff to knaw when to start that sort o' tomfu-lishness he won't have gumtion enough to knaw when to stop, that's fer certin.

When the time come fer me to go to the golf again, Ned Annaferd and Lias Buzzacott went along too. They axed me if they might, and I said they cude and welcome. When a feller starts makin' a fule of hiszell he gener'ly do's the thing proper. I was turrable plaised at the time that they shude come and zee me play golf.

I'd give vive pound now, if they cude 'a-bin hundred mile away. If Ned and Lias had'n bin there to watch I might 'a-bin able to keep it dark. But from what I can zee aw't, they waun' be satisfied till everybody fer tain mile around have yeard how Jan Stewer played golf.

Mr Bamfield was there, ready and waitin' when us got to the plaace, and he had his wive along with 'n.

'You daun' mind my missis comin' around, do 'ee, Jan?' he saith. 'Her ab'm played a lot, and I thought her'd be more about your mark, 'cus her's only larnin'.'

'Coorse, I said I was very plaised, and so I was, 'cus Mrs Bamfield's a very nice laady. But all the zame, I thought 'twas like Tommy's chick to zay her'd be about my mark. I said to mezell, 'I'll let you zee all about my mark in a minute, ole Cock o' the Walk.' I winkid across to Ned, as gude as to zay, 'You 'old 'ard, and zee.' And ole Ned he nodded back, as much as to zay, 'I be lookin'.'

Tommy had his bag o' tools, and he'd fetched along another bagful fer me to lug about. I did'n zee no sainse in taking along that lot, 'cus they was a tidy heft, so I said one wude be sufficient vor me and I'd laive the rest behind. But he was very aiger that I shude take the lot, so I did'n make no more bones about it, speshly as Mrs Bamfield had got a bagful to carr'.

Tommy said I mus' larn the names of all the sticks, and he tooked 'em out from the bag one to a time and showed 'em to me. I can't mind all their names now, but the chap with the big nob was the driver, and there was wan called a masher, and a nibble-it, and a putter. Quare lookin' sample they was, take 'em wan with another.

I'll tell 'ee what they did look like, fer all the gude in the world. They lookid like a set o' weedin' tools fer the garden.

'Anybody wude think us was gwain cuttin' dashels,' I says.

I reckoned zomebody must 'a-bin usin' 'em purty bad, 'cus they was twisted all shapes. Speshly the nibble-it feller. Properly out o' the straight he was. The hannle was all right, but the li'l hoe on the end was hawful crooked. I spause Tommy thought any ole thing wude do fer me, but I did'n complain about it, 'cus I reckoned I shude'n require to use more'n wan o' the tools.

When us got to the startin' paust Mr Bamfield said, 'Now, Jan, I be gwain to drive off, and you take pa'ticler notice how I do's it.'

And then I understood him to zay he was gwain to make tay.

'Bit early fer that, maister, id'n it?' I says. 'I've only recently had me dinner.'

Caw, did'n 'um laaf! Then I found that what he called makin' tay was heapin' up thik handful o' durt what I told 'ee about, to rest the ball on.

'You haves yer driver vor this strike,' he says. So he tooked out the stick with the nob at the bottom, and then he started gwain droo all they old crams again, pretendin' to get ready fer zummin wonderful, 'itchin' his veet, and wrigglin' his tail and swingin' his arms around to make sure they was in gear. Then he let rip to the ball and fetched 'n a turrable scat. Mind you, I will zay he sent 'n a doost of a way; but I considered I cude better it when it come to my turn.

Then Mrs Bamfield had a go to it. Her went droo all the zame antics, but her did'n zend the ball much more 'n half the distance. Still, I had to zay that was very gude fer a laady, 'cus I did'n want vor her to get down-couraged.

'Now, Jan, you have a try,' says Tommy; and he let me have a ball to scat. 'Bout the size of a pullet's egg he was, only round, o' coorse. I putt 'n down on the floor.

'Better tay 'en up,' he says. 'I'll make a tay for 'ee.'

'No, let 'n bide as he is,' I says. 'I can hat 'n all-so-well there.'

I did'n mind scattin' a ball about to amuse 'em, but I wad'n gwain to play makin' mud pies to plaise nobody. And I thought to mezell, 'I ban't gwain droo no stoobid ole antics, nuther. You said I was to watch you, now you watch me.'

So I ups with me driver and I let go wan blow to thik ball which I considered wude scat 'n across dree parishes. In fac', I putt so much force behind 'n I swinged mezell right off me feet, 'cus I was determined to send the li'l toad to Jericho. Lias was stood zix voot behind me, but he only ducked his haid just in the nick o' time. Another second and I'd have scat out his brains with my stick.

'Where have that wan gone to?' I said, when I got back.

'He ab'm started yet,' says Tommy.

'What do 'ee mean, not started?'

Caw, I'm jiggered! When I come to look, there was the blessid ball, zac'ly where I putt 'n to. I had'n moved the li'l begger.

'Mean to zay I missed'n?' I says.

'You did'n acsh'ly miss 'n, Jan,' says Ned. 'You hat 'n about a voot too high up.'

'Get on with 'ee,' I says. ''Twad'n nothin' like that. Cude'n 'a-bin much more'n a hair's breath.'

'Try again, Jan,' says Tommy.

'Wait a minute,' says Lias. 'Let me get behind a tree.'

'Don't go quite so hard this time,' says Tommy. But I reckoned I knawed what he was up to. He did'n want fer me to send my ball beyond he's; so I hat 'n a bit harder if anything. But I didn't have me stick hold hardly tight enough and he slipped right out of me hand. If Ned Annaferd had'n jumped up in the air smarter than he have fer the last vorty year, 'twude 'a-ketched he a wop in the leg. He'd have knawed which leg 'twas too, vor thikky stick flied a guns-hot bevore he valled to ground.

'Yer 'old 'ard, Jan,' he says. 'I thought you was playin' golf, not Aunt Zally.'

'I'm gwain to sit on the ball,' says Lias. 'That's the safest place, looks-so. Jan ab'm titched that wan.'

I'm bothered if it wad'n true, too. There the ball was, same's ever, lookin' up to me so innocent, as if he did'n know I'd ever had a stick in me 'and.

Mr Bamfield said, 'You mus' keep yer eye on the ball, Jan.'

'I shude if I was you, Jan,' says Lias. 'You'll be sure it won't get hurted, there.'

'And you mus' keep yer haid still, likewise.'

'If Lias had kep' his still,' says Ned, 'He'd have had it knocked off by now.'

'Many worse things than that might hap'm,' I said, 'cus between you and me, I was gettin' a bit wopsy. I knowed very well 'twas only Mrs Bamfield's gude manners was keepin' her from laafin' right out; and the same with Tommy. The other two had'n got no gude manners, and they was bustin' their sides.

'I zee what's the matter, Mr Bamfield,' says Lias. 'You hav'n gived Mr Stewer a proper outfit. You've only let 'n have a driver. What he wants is a conducter as well.'

'He'd need to be a lightnin' conducter to keep out o' the way o' that stick,' says Ned.

However, I went and got me driver back again, and I let go to thik ball with a whack which shude have zend 'n to Halifax. But it did'n turn 'en auver. It did'n touch 'en. You wude'n believe it was possible, wude 'ee? But 'tis true as I'm sot yer. There was the ball, and there was a long stick with a gurt nob, and there was me, and do you think I cude shift the little baiste? I swished at en' with all me might and he lied there laafin' at me. Then I lost me temper and started swingin' me stick like the old wumman baitin' carpets. Zix goes I had, wan arter t'other, and I did'n make no more differ'nce to the ball than if he wad'n there. But if Mrs Bamfield had'n been stood close handy I'd have called he somethin' that wude have made 'n bury hiszell in the ground. I was bustin' to zay it, and I *did* zay a bit of it. And then her laafed, manners or no manners.

'You'd better putt'n up on a tay, Jan,' says Tommy. ''Tis proper thing to do.'

So he putt down a handful o' durt and rised the ball up a bit. And this time I hat 'n a buster. I knowed I had 'cus I heard the crack.

'Did anybody zee where that wan went to?' I says, ''cus I did'n.'

'You wude'n be likely to,' says Lias, 'without you'd got eyes in yer tail. If you stap back you'll putt yer voot on it.'

He was right. I turned around and there the ball was, not a tailor's yard away; and the oppozyte derection to what he shude 'a-bin. How do he do it, can anybody tell me?

'Better have that wan again,' says Tommy, and he trigged 'n up on the tay wance more.

By this time I was beginnin' to wonder whether I was quite so clever as I thought I was. I wished with all me 'art and zaul I had'n had quite so much to zay about what I was gwain to do. I 'ope 'twill be a lesson to me for the future.

'Let me show 'ee how to hold yer club the right way,' says Tommy. And I let 'n to, like a lamb. Vive minutes bevore I shude have considered me awn way was best. But I'm jiggered if thik li'l ball had'n took the stuffin' out o' me.

This time I did manage to knock 'n vore a bit, but 'twad'n half the distance of Mrs Bamfield's, let alone Tommy's.

'That's more like it,' he says. ''Tis in the right derection, anyway. Bring yer bag along, and knock 'n a bit furder.'

So us walked to where my ball was lied on the grass, and Mr Bamfield said I must have wan o' the garden tools this time. I started off back.

'Where be gwain?' he says.

'For a handful o' durt,' I said. 'I shall have a tay this time.'

But that id'n allowed in the rules, don't seem so. You can only have a tay for the fust start off. Arter that you mus' knock the ball wherever he lies to. And I can tell you, he lies in some very vunny places, zometimes. Mine did, anyway. 'Twude be redec'lus to zay a li'l white ball can think for hiszell and choose what place he shall creep into, but I'll make a bet, if there *was* a bit of a hole in the ground or any sort of ockerd place where he cude squaise in, he'd get in there, zome'ow. He was in wan now.

I dreads to tell 'ee what happened next. Tommy said I must have a go at 'n with the masher, so I did. Matter o' fact, I had vive goes at 'n, bevore ever I touched 'n at all, and when I did fetch 'n a scat, to-last, he did'n go a bit the way I was lookin'. He flied up in the air like a burd and come down in a pit full o' sand. And you try to knock a ball out of a heap o' sand with a crooked hoe and zee what 'tis like. I was for pickin' out the li'l toad and restin' him on the hard ground. But you muzzen do that, by all accounts. 'Where he lies to!' That's the rules.

'Well, then,' I said, 'they did'n ought to go leavin' ditches about like this. I shude think, considerin' all the money they've spent on the place, they cude afford to fill this one in, and putt a bit o' turn auver it.'

My, did'n Tommy Bamfield laaf!

'That's putt there a-purpose,' he says, 'to make it more difficult.'

'I shude think 'tis plenty difficult enough,' I says, 'without any making.'

'Ullaw!' sayd Ned, 'I fancy zomebody have changed his chune. I understood 'twas cheel's play.'

'That's right,' I says. 'I've bin waitin' vor that. You come and have a try at it, and you'll do the same as I'm gwain to do.'

'What's that, then?'

'Why, tell a differ'nt tale,' I says.

I wude'n like to tell 'ee how many whacks I had to the ball bevore I got 'n out from the sand, nor how much o' the sand I shifted in the transaction. I'm thankful to zay the rest of 'em got a gudish bit of the sand down backs o' their necks, and Lias got a mouthful, which made 'n ferget what he was gwain to zay.

I got my li'l joke out o' that lot, too. The very fust whack I give the ball, instaid of he coming out, as I ordained for 'en to, he went right in and buried hiszell. They all started to laff, but I said: 'Well,' I said, 'there's wan thing I can zay. I *can* boast that I hat my ball right out o' sight, and that's more than eether of you can.'

Ned Annaferd said, 'I thought this was golf you was doing, Jan, not badger-digging.'

They ditches be called 'bunkums' so I understand, and a very gude name for 'em too. There's dizzens of 'em about, all auver the plaace, and I shude think, fust and last, I must have got in every wan of 'em at laist twice. Every time I hat a ball, I eetherways missed 'n altogether, or else he went flyin' off lookin' vor a bunkum. If he cude'n vind a bunkum he'd go down a rabbut-'awl, or else in a vuz-bush. If there'd been a hen's nest about I'll make a bet he'd have crept into that one and pretended he was a winedot's egg.

However, arter a vew more scats us come to the smooth grassen plat with the hole in the middle. That's what they calls a green, and you've got to make yer ball go in the li'l pot. If it had only been a hole where he wad'n suppaused to go, I cude have got mine in as aisy as winky. All I'd have to do wude be to shut me eyes and give 'n a scat, and in he'd go. But do you think he'd go in when I wanted vor 'en to? Not he wude'n. He'd go around 'en, or he'd jump auver the tap of 'en, or he'd go to the edge and keen down auver the side. He'd do any mortle thing, seps go een.

When I did get 'n in, to-last, they said I'd had zeb'm and twenty knocks for thik hole, from start to finish. Mrs Bamfield had zeb'm, and Tommy had vive.

Lias said they ought to reckon it the zame as they do cricket, and then I shude be the winner, aisy. Ned Annaferd was figgering with a pencil and a bit o' paaper.

'What be you up top?' I said.

'I was jis' doin' a bit o' 'rithmetic,' he says. 'How many o' these-yer holes did you say there was, Mr Bamfield?'

'Eighteen, Ned. But us waun't be able to do 'em all to-day. Us'll take a short cut.'

'That's eighteen times zeb'm-an'-twenty,' says Ned. 'Jan said las' wik you tooked zempty-nine, and he was gwain to show you the way to do it proper. As near as I can work it out, at the rate he've gone on already, 'twill take he vower hunderd and eighty-zix. So I propose he shude give us a wik's notice when he'm coming towards the last 'ole, and then us'll come auver and zee 'en finish.'

10

BEGINNER'S LUCK

by A. G. Macdonell

A. G. MACDONELL'S hilarious description of a village cricket match in his classic book, *England, Their England* (1933), is probably one of the most authologised pieces in collections featuring either sport or humour! Despite the well-deserved fame of this story, Macdonell, who was actually a Scot born in Aberdeen, believed that the episode in the book which dealt with golf was an even funnier and more accurate piece of writing.

The author in fact played golf about as well and as often as he played cricket – and with much the same infectious enthusiasm – and one has the feeling that there is more than a little personal experience in some of the adventures that occur to his hero, Donald Cameron, in *England, Their England*. Not that one would be unhappy experiencing the kind of luck which befalls Donald in the pages which follow.

BEGINNER'S LUCK

A few days after his curious experience on the cricket field, Donald's attention was drawn away from the problem of the Englishman's attitude towards his national game by a chance paragraph in a leading newspaper on the subject of Golf. And golf was a matter of grave temptation to Donald at this period of his life.

Both Sir Ethelred Ormerode, MP, and Sir Ludovic Phibbs, MP, had invited him to a day's golf at one or other of the large clubs near London to which they belonged; but Donald had made excuses to avoid acceptance, for the following reason. He had played no golf since he had been a lad of eighteen at Aberdeen, and as he had not enough money to join a club in the south and play regularly, he was unwilling to resurrect an ancient passion which he had no means of gratifying. Up to the age of eighteen golf had been a religion to him far more inspiring and appealing than the dry dogmatics of the various sections of the Presbyterian Church which wrangled in those days so enthusiastically in the North-East of Scotland. Since that time, of course, there has been a notable reunion of the sections and public wrangling has perforce come to an end, an end regretted so passionately that the phrase 'a peace-maker' in that part of the world is rapidly acquiring the sense of a busy-body or a spoil-sport. As one ancient soldier of the Faith, whose enthusiasm for the Word was greater than his knowledge of it, was recently heard to observe bitterly into the depths of his patriarchal beard, 'Isn't it enough for them to have been promised the Kingdom of Heaven, without they must poke their disjaskit nebs into Buchan and the Mearns?'

But whatever the rights and wrongs of the once indignant and now cooing Churches, it is a fact that Donald before the War was more interested in golf than in religion, and a handicap of plus one when he was seventeen had marked him out as a coming man. But first the War and then the work of farming the Mains of Balspindie had put an end to all that, and Donald was reluctant to awaken the dragon.

But one day he happened to read in one of the most famous newspapers in the world the following paragraph in a column written by 'Our Golf Correspondent':

'Our recent defeat at the hands of the stern and wild Caledonians was, no doubt, demnition horrid, as our old friend would have said, and had it not been for the amazing series of flukes by which the veteran Bernardo, now well advanced in decrepitude, not only managed to hang on to the metaphorical coat-tails of his slashing young adversary, but even to push his nose in front on the last green, the score of the Sassenachs would have been as blank as their faces. For their majestic leader was snodded on the fourteenth green, and even the Dumkins and the Podder of the team, usually safe cards, met their Bannockburn. And that was that. The only consolation for this unexpected "rewersal" lies in the fact that the Northerners consisted almost entirely of what are called Anglo-Scots, domiciled in England and products of English golf. For there is no doubt that the balance of golfing power has shifted to the south, and England is now the real custodian of the ancient traditions of the game. Which, as a consolation prize, is all wery capital.'

Donald read this through carefully several times, for it seemed to be a matter of importance to him and his work. He had seen, at very close quarters, the English engaged upon their ancient, indigenous national pastime, and he had been unable to make head or tail of it.

But it was worth while going out of his way to see how they treated another nation's national game which, according to the golf correspondent, they had mastered perfectly and had, as it were, adopted and nationalised.

The matter was easily arranged, and, on the following Sunday, he was picked up at the corner of Royal Avenue and King's Road by Sir Ludovic Phibbs in a Rolls-Royce limousine car. Sir Ludovic was wearing a superb fur coat and was wrapped in a superb fur rug. On the way down to Cedar Park, the venue of the day's golf, Sir Ludovic talked a good deal about the scandal of the dole. It appeared to be his view that everyone who took the dole ought to be shot in order to teach them not to slack. The solution of the whole trouble was the abolition of Trades Unionism and harder work all round, including Saturday afternoons and a half-day Sundays. This theme lasted most of the journey, and Donald was not called upon to contribute more than an occasional monosyllable.

Cedar Park is one of the newest of the great golf clubs which are ringed round the north, west, and south of London in such profusion, and what is now the club-house had been in earlier centuries the mansion of a venerable line of marquesses. High taxation had completed the havoc in the venerable finances which had begun in the Georgian and Victorian generations by high gambling, and the entire estate was sold shortly after the War by the eleventh marquess to a man who had, during it, made an enormous fortune by a most ingenious dodge. For, alone with the late Lord Kitchener, he had realised in August and September of 1914 that the War was going to be a very long business, thus providing ample opportunities for very big business, and that before it was over it would require a British

Army of millions and millions of soldiers. Having first of all taken the precaution of getting himself registered as a man who was indispensable to the civil life of the nation during the great Armageddon, for at the outbreak of hostilities he was only thirty-one years of age, and, in order to be on the safe side, having had himself certified by a medical man as suffering from short sight, varicose veins, a weak heart, and incipient lung trouble, he set himself upon his great task of cornering the world's supply of rum. By the middle of 1917 he had succeeded, and in 1920 he paid ninety-three thousand pounds for Cedar Park, and purchased in addition a house in Upper Brook Street, a hunting-box near Melton, a two-thousand-ton motor-yacht, Lochtarig Castle, Inverness-shire, and the long leases of three luxurious flats in Mayfair in which to entertain, without his wife knowing, by day or night, his numerous lady friends. He was, of course, knighted for his public services during the War. It was not until 1925 that the rum-knight shot himself to avoid an absolutely certain fourteen years for fraudulent conversion, and Cedar Park was acquired by a syndicate of Armenian sportsmen for the purpose of converting it into a country club.

An enormous man in a pale-blue uniform tricked out with thick silver cords and studded with cartwheel silver buttons, opened the door of the car and bowed Sir Ludovic, and a little less impressively, Donald Cameron into the club-house. Donald was painfully conscious that his grey flannel trousers bagged at the knee and that his old blue 1914 golfing-coat had a shine at one elbow and a hole at the other.

The moment he entered the club-house a superb spectacle met his dazzled gaze. It was not the parquet floor, on which his nail-studded shoes squeaked loudly, or the marble columns, or the voluptuous paintings on the ceiling, or the gilt-framed mirrors on the walls, or the chandeliers of a thousand crystals, or even the palms in their gilt pots and synthetic earth, that knocked him all of a heap. It was the group of golfers that was standing in front of the huge fire-place. There were purple jumpers and green jumpers and yellow jumpers and tartan jumpers; there were the biggest, the baggiest, the brightest plus-fours that ever dulled the lustre of a peacock's tail; there were the rosiest of lips, the gayest of cheeks, and flimsiest of silk stockings, and the orangest of finger-nails and probably, if the truth were known, of toe-nails too; there were waves of an unbelievable permanence and lustre; there were jewels, on the men as well as on the women, and foot-long jade and amber cigarette-holders and foot-long cigars with glistening cummerbunds; and there was laughter and gaiety and much bending, courtier-like, from the waist, and much raising of girlish, kohl-fringed eyes, and a great chattering. Donald felt like a navvy, and when, in his agitation, he dropped his clubs with a resounding clash upon the floor and everyone stopped talking and looked at him, he wished he was dead. Another pale-blue-and-silver giant picked up the clubs, held them out at arm's length and examined them in disdainful astonishment – for after years of disuse they were very rusty – and said coldly, 'Clubs go into the locker-room, sir,' and Donald squeaked his way across the parquet after him amid a profound silence.

The locker-room was full of young gentlemen who were discarding their jumpers – which certainly competed with Mr Shelley's idea of Life Staining the White Radiance of Eternity – in favour of brown leather jerkins fastened up the front with that singular arrangement which is called a zipper. Donald edged in furtively, hazily watched the flunkey lay the clubs down upon a bench, and then fled in panic through the nearest open door and found himself suddenly in a wire-netted enclosure which was packed with a dense throng of caddies. The caddies were just as surprised by his appearance in their midst as the elegant ladies and gentlemen in the lounge had been by the fall of the clubs, and a deathly stillness once again paralysed Donald.

He backed awkwardly out of the enclosure, bouncing off caddy after caddy like a cork coming over a rock-studded sluice, and was brought up short at last by what seemed to be a caddy rooted immovably in the ground. Two desperate back-ward lunges failed to dislodge the obstacle and Donald turned and found it was the wall of the professional's shop. The caddies, and worse still, an exquisitely beautiful young lady with a cupid's-bow mouth and practically no skirt on at all, who had just emerged from the shop, watched him with profound interest. Scarlet in the face, he rushed past the radiant beauty, and hid himself in the darkest corner of the shop and pretended to be utterly absorbed in a driver which he picked out at random from the rack. Rather to his surprise, and greatly to his relief, no one molested him with up-to-date, go-getting salesmanship, and in a few minutes he had pulled himself together and was able to look round and face the world.

Suddenly he gave a start. Something queer was going on inside him. He sniffed the air once, and then again, and then the half-forgotten past came rushing to him across the wasted years. The shining rows of clubs, the boxes of balls, the scent of leather and rubber and gripwax and pitch, the club-makers filing away over the vices and polishing and varnishing and splicing and binding, the casual members waggling a club here and there, the professional listening courteously to tales of apocryphal feats, all the old familiar scenes of his youth came back to him. It was eleven years since he had played a game of golf, thirteen years since he had bought a club. Thirteen wasted years. Dash it, thought Donald, damn it, blast it, I can't afford a new club – I don't want a new club, but I'm going to buy a new club. He spoke diffidently to one of the assistants who was passing behind him, and enquired the price of the drivers.

'It's a new lot just finished, sir,' said the assistant, 'and I'm not sure of the price. I'll ask Mr Glennie.'

Mr Glennie was the professional himself. The great man, who was talking to a member, or rather was listening to a member's grievances against his luck, a ritual which occupies a large part of a professional's working day, happened to over-hear the assistant, and he said over his shoulder in the broadest of broad Scottish accents, 'They're fufty-twa shullin' and cheap at that'.

Donald started back. Two pounds twelve for a driver! Things had changed indeed since the days when the great Archie Simpson had sold him a brassy, brand-new, bright yellow, refulgent driver with a lovely whippy shaft, for five shillings and nine-pence.

His movement of Aberdonian horror brought him out of the dark corner into the sunlight which was streaming through the window, and it was the professional's turn to jump.

'It's Master Donald!' he exclaimed. 'Yes mind me, Master Donald – Jim Glennie, assistant that was at Glenavie to Tommy Anderson that went to the States?'

'Glennie!' cried Donald, a subtle warm feeling suddenly invading his body, and he grasped the professional's huge red hand.

'Man!' cried the latter, 'but I'm glad to see ye. How lang is't sin' we used to ding awa at each other roon' Glenavie? Man, it must be years and years. And fit's aye deein' wi' yer game? Are ye plus sax or seeven?'

'Glennie,' said Donald sadly, 'I haven't touched a club since those old days. This is the first time I've set foot in a professional's shop since you took me that time to see Alec Marling at Balgownie the day before the War broke out.'

'Eh, man, but you're a champion lost,' and the professional shook his head mournfully.

'But, Glennie,' went on Donald, 'where did you learn that fine Buchan accent? You never used to talk like that. Is it since you came south that you've picked it up?'

The big professional looked a little shamefaced and drew Donald back into the dark corner.

'It's good for trade,' he whispered in the pure English of Inverness. 'They like a Scot to be real Scottish. They think it makes a man what they call "a character". God knows why, but there it is. So I just humour them by talking like a Guild Street carter who's having a bit of back-chat with an Aberdeen fish-wife. It makes the profits something extraordinary.'

'Hi! Glennie, you old swindler,' shouted a stoutish, red-faced man who was smoking a big cigar and wearing a spectroscopic suit of tweeds. 'How much do you want to sting me for this putter?'

'Thirty-twa shullin' and saxpence, Sir Walter,' replied Glennie over his shoulder, 'but ye'll be wastin' yer siller, for neither that club nor any ither wull bring ye doon below eighteen.'

A delighted laugh from a group of men behind Sir Walter greeted this sally.

'You see,' whispered Glennie, 'he'll buy it and he'll tell his friends that I tried to dissuade him, and they'll all agree that I'm a rare old character, and they'll all come and buy too.'

'But fifty-two shillings for a driver!' said Donald. 'Do you mean to say they'll pay that?'

'Yes, of course they will. They'll pay anything so long as it's more than any other professional at any other club charges them. That's the whole secret. Those drivers there aren't a new set at all. They're the same set as I was asking forty-eight shillings for last week-end, but I heard during the week from a friend who keeps an eye open for me, that young Jock Robbie over at Addingdale Manor had put his drivers and brassies up from forty-six shillings to fifty, the dirty young dog. Not that I blame him. It's a new form of commercial competition, Master Donald, a sort of inverted price-cutting. Na, na, Muster Hennessey,' he broke into his trade voice again, 'ye dinna want ony new clubs. Ye're playin' brawly with yer auld yins. Still, if ye want to try yon spoon, tak it oot and play a couple of roons wi' it, and if ye dinna like it put it back.'

He turned to Donald again.

'That's a sure card down here. They always fall for it. They take the club and tell their friends that I've given it to them on trial because I'm not absolutely certain that it will suit their game, and they never bring it back. Not once. Did you say you wanted a driver, Master Donald?'

'Not at fifty-two shillings,' said Donald with a smile.

Glennie indignantly waved away the suggestion.

'You shall have your pick of the shop at cost price,' he said, and then, looking furtively round and lowering his voice until it was almost inaudible, he breathed in Donald's ear, 'Fifteen and six.'

Donald chose a beautiful driver, treading on air all the while and feeling eighteen years of age, and then Sir Ludovic Phibbs came into the shop.

'Ah! There you are, Cameron,' he said genially; 'there are only two couples in front of us now. Are you ready? Good morning, Glennie, you old shark. There's no use trying to swing the lead over Mr Cameron. He's an Aberdonian himself.'

[111]

As Donald went out, Glennie thrust a box of balls under his arm and whispered, 'For old time's sake!'

On the first tee Sir Ludovic introduced him to the other two players who were going to make up the match. One was a Mr Wollaston, a clean-shaven, intelligent, large, prosperous-looking man of about forty, and the other was a Mr Gyles, a very dark man, with a toothbrush moustache and a most impressive silence. Both were stockbrokers.

'Now,' said Sir Ludovic heartily, 'I suggest that we play a four-ball foursome, Wollaston and I against you two, on handicap, taking our strokes from the course, five bob corners, half a crown for each birdie, a dollar an eagle, a bob best ball and a bob aggregate and a bob a putt. What about that?'

'Good!' said Mr Wollaston. Mr Gyles nodded, while Donald, who had not understood a single word except the phrase 'four-ball foursome' – and that was incorrect – mumbled a feeble affirmative. The stakes sounded enormous, and the reference to birds of the air sounded mysterious, but he obviously could not raise any objections.

When it was his turn to drive at the first tee, he selected a spot for his tee and tapped it with the toe of his driver. Nothing happened. He looked at his elderly caddy and tapped the ground again. Again nothing happened.

'Want a peg, Cameron?' called out Sir Ludovic.

'Oh no, it's much too early,' protested Donald, under the impression that he was being offered a drink. Everyone laughed ecstatically at this typically Scottish flash of wit, and the elderly caddy lurched forward with a loathsome little contrivance of blue and white celluloid which he offered to his employer. Donald shuddered. They'd be giving him a rubber tee with a tassel in a minute, or lending him a golf-bag with tripod legs. He teed his ball on a pinch of sand with a dexterous twist of his fingers and thumb amid an incredulous silence.

Donald played the round in a sort of daze. After a few holes of uncertainty, much of his old skill came back, and he reeled off fairly good figures. He had a little difficulty with his elderly caddy at the beginning of the round, for, on asking that functionary to hand him 'the iron', he received the reply, 'Which number, sir?' and the following dialogue ensued:

'Which number what?' faltered Donald.

'Which number iron?'

'Er – just the iron?'

'But it must have a number, sir.'

'Why must it?'

'All irons have numbers.'

'But I've only one.'

'Only a number one?'

'No. Only one.'

'Only one what, sir?'

'One iron!' exclaimed Donald, feeling that this music-hall turn might go on for a long time and must be already holding up the entire course.

The elderly caddy at last appreciated the deplorable state of affairs. He looked grievously shocked and said in a reverent tone:

'Mr Fumbledon has eleven.'

'Eleven what?' enquired the startled Donald.

'Eleven irons.'

After this revelation of Mr Fumbledon's greatness, Donald took 'the iron' and topped the ball hard along the ground. The caddy sighed deeply.

Throughout the game Donald never knew what the state of the match was, for the other three, who kept complicated tables upon the backs of envelopes, reckoned solely in cash. Thus, when Donald once timidly asked his partner how they stood, the taciturn Mr Gyles consulted his envelope and replied shortly, after a brief calculation, 'You're up three dollars and a tanner.'

Donald did not venture to ask again, and he knew nothing more about the match until they were ranged in front of the bar in the club-room, when Sir Ludovic and Mr Wollaston put down the empty glasses which had, a moment ago, contained double pink gins, ordered a refill of the four glasses, and then handed over to the bewildered Donald the sum of one pound sixteen and six.

Lunch was an impressive affair. It was served in a large

room, panelled in white and gold with a good deal of artificial marble scattered about the walls, by a staff of bewitching young ladies in black frocks, white aprons and caps, and black silk stockings. Bland wine-stewards drifted hither and thither, answering to Christian names and accepting orders and passing them on to subordinates. Corks popped, the scent of the famous club fish-pie mingled itself with all the perfumes of Arabia and Mr Coty, smoke arose from rose-tipped ciga-rettes, and the rattle of knives and forks played an orchestral accompaniment to the sound of many voices, mostly silvery, like April rain, and full of girlish gaiety.

Sir Ludovic insisted on being host, and ordered Donald's half-pint of beer and double whiskies for himself and Mr Gyles. Mr Wollaston, pleading a diet and the strict orders of Carlsbad medicos, produced a bottle of Berncastler out of a small brown handbag, and polished it off in capital style.

The meal itself consisted of soup, the famous fish-pie, a fricassee of chicken, saddle of mutton or sirloin of roast beef, sweet, savoury, and cheese, topped off with four of the biggest glasses of hunting port that Donald had ever seen. Conversa-tion at lunch was almost entirely about the dole. The party then went back to the main club-room where Mr Wollaston firmly but humorously pushed Sir Ludovic into a very deep chair, and insisted upon taking up the running with four coffees and four double kümmels. Then after a couple of rubbers of bridge, at which Donald managed to win a few shillings, they sallied out to play a second round. The golf was only indifferent in the afternoon. Sir Ludovic complained that, owing to the recrudescence of what he mysteriously called 'the old trouble', he was finding it very difficult to focus the ball clearly, and Mr Wollaston kept on over-swinging so violently that he fell over once and only just saved himself on several other occasions, and Mr Gyles developed a fit of socketing that soon became a menace to the course, causing, as it did, acute nervous shocks to a retired major-general whose sunlit nose only escaped by a miracle, and a bevy of beauty that was admiring, for some reason, the play of a well-known actor-manager.

So after eight holes the afternoon round was abandoned by

common consent, and they walked back to the club-house for more bridge and much-needed refreshment. Donald was handed seventeen shillings as his inexplicable winnings over the eight holes. Later on, Sir Ludovic drove, or rather Sir Ludovic's chauffeur drove, Donald back to the corner of King's Road and Royal Avenue. On the way back, Sir Ludovic talked mainly about the dole.

Seated in front of the empty grate in his bed-sitting-room, Donald counted his winnings and reflected that golf had changed a great deal since he had last played it.

11

A CADDY'S DIARY

by Ring Lardner

RING LARDNER was the first major American author to employ his pen writing humour about golf, and since the early 1930's his influence has been evident in magazines and newspapers through the nation. A former sports reporter, Lardner leapt to national fame when he began writing short stories which drew on his observation of matches and his conversations with players. Paying tribute to him, Columbia University critic William Bridgwater said recently, 'Lardner's pungent idiom of the sports world has made him a much-imitated master of tough and sardonic humour.'

The only sport that Lardner himself played was golf, where it was said he used his wit as much as his skill with the clubs to beat opponents. He had first learned about the game caddying for his father, and this fact gives added relish to the story which follows. Equally, I think, it vividly demonstrates *why* Lardner enjoys such a high reputation as a writer of humorous short stories.

A CADDY'S DIARY

Wed. Apr. 12.

I am 16 of age and am a caddy at the Pleasant View Golf Club but only temporary as I expect to soon land a job some wheres as asst pro as my game is good enough now to be a pro but to young looking. My pal Joe Bean also says I have not got enough swell head to make a good pro but suppose that will come in time, Joe is a wise cracker.

But first will put down how I come to be writeing this diary, we have got a member name Mr Colby who writes articles in the newspapers and I hope for his sakes that he is a better writer then he plays golf but any way I cadded for him a good many times last yr and today he was out for the first time this yr and I cadded for him and we got talking about this in that and something was mentioned in regards to the golf articles by Alex Laird that comes out every Sun in the paper Mr Colby writes his articles for so I asked Mr Colby did he know how much Laird got paid for the articles and he said he did not know but supposed that Laird had to split 50–50 with who ever wrote the articles for him. So I said don't he write the articles himself and Mr Colby said why no he guessed not.

Laird may be a master mind in regards to golf he said, but that is no sign he can write about it as very few men can write decent let alone a pro. Writeing is a nag.

How do you learn it I asked him.

Well he said read what other people writes and study them and write things yourself, and maybe you will get on to the nag and maybe you wont.

Well Mr Colby I said do you think I could get on to it?

Why he said smileing I did not know that was your ambition to be a writer.

Not exactly was my reply, but I am going to be a golf pro myself and maybe some day I will get good enough so as the papers will want I should write them articles and if I can learn to write them myself why I will not have to hire another writer and split with them.

Well said Mr Colby smileing you have certainly got the right temperament for a pro, they are all big hearted fellows.

But listen Mr Colby I said if I want to learn it would not do me no good to copy down what other writers have wrote, what I would have to do would be write things out of my own head.

That is true said Mr Colby.

Well I said what could I write about?

Well said Mr Colby why don't you keep a diary and every night after your supper set down and write what happened that day and write who you cadded for and what they done only leave me out of it. And you can write down what people say and what you think and etc., it will be the best kind of practice for you, and once in a wile you can bring me your writeings and I will tell you the truth if they are good or rotten.

So that is how I come to be writeing this diary is so as I can get some practice writeing and maybe if I keep at it long enough I can get on to the nag.

Friday, Apr. 14.

We been haveing Apr. showers for a couple days and nobody out on the course so they has been nothing happen that I could write down in my diary but dont want to leave it go to long or will never learn the trick so will try and write a few lines about a caddys life and some of our members and etc.

Well I and Joe Bean is the 2 oldest caddys in the club and I been cadding now for 5 yrs and quit school 3 yrs ago tho my mother did not like it for me to quit but my father said he can read and write and figure so what is the use in keeping him there any longer as greek and latin dont get you no credit at the grocer, so they lied about my age to the trunce officer and I been cadding every yr from March till Nov and the rest of the winter I work around Heismans store in the village.

Dureing the time I am cadding I genally always manage to play at lease 9 holes a day myself on wk days and some times 18 and am never more then 2 or 3 over par figures on our course but it is a cinch.

I played the engineers course 1 day last summer in 75 which is some golf and some of our members who has been playing 20 yrs would give their right eye to play as good as myself.

I use to play around with our pro Jack Andrews till I got so as I could beat him pretty near every time we played and now he wont play with me no more, he is not a very good player for a pro but they claim he is a good teacher. Personly I think golf teachers is a joke tho I am glad people is suckers enough to fall for it as I expect to make my liveing that way. We have got a member Mr Dunham who must of took 500 lessons in the past 3 yrs and when he starts to shoot he trys to remember all the junk Andrews has learned him and he gets dizzy and they is no telling where the ball will go and about the safest place to stand when he is shooting is between he and the hole.

I dont beleive the club pays Andrews much salery but of course he makes pretty fair money giveing lessons but his best graft is a 3 some which he plays 2 and 3 times a wk with Mr Perdue and Mr Lewis and he gives Mr Lewis a stroke a hole and they genally break some wheres near even but Mr Perdue made a 83 one time so he thinks that is his game so he insists on playing Jack even, well they always play for $5.00 a hole and Andrews makes $20.00 to $30.00 per round and if he wanted to cut loose and play his best he could make $50.00 to $60.00 per round but a couple of wallops like that and Mr Perdue might get cured so Jack figures a small stedy income is safer.

I have got a pal name Joe Bean and we pal around together

as he is about my age and he says some comical things and some times will wisper some thing comical to me wile we are cadding and it is all I can do to help from laughing out loud, that is one of the first things a caddy has got to learn is never laugh out loud only when a member makes a joke. How ever on the days when theys ladies on the course I dont get a chance to caddy with Joe because for some reason another the woman folks dont like Joe to caddy for them wile on the other hand they are always after me tho I am no Othello for looks or do I seek their flavors, in fact it is just the opp and I try to keep in the back ground when the fair sex appears on the seen as cadding for ladies means you will get just so much money and no more as theys no chance of them loosning up. As Joe says the rule against tipping is the only rule the woman folks keeps.

Theys one lady how ever who I like to caddy for as she looks like Lillian Gish and it is a pleasure to just look at her and I would caddy for her for nothing tho it is hard to keep your eye on the ball when you are cadding for this lady, her name is Mrs Doane.

Sat. Apr. 15.

This was a long day and am pretty well wore out but must not get behind in my writeing practice. I and Joe carried all day for Mr Thomas and Mr Blake. Mr Thomas is the vice president of one of the big banks down town and he always slips you a $1.00 extra per round but believe me you earn it cadding for Mr Thomas, there is just 16 clubs in his bag includeing 5 wood clubs tho he has not used the wood in 3 yrs but says he has got to have them along in case his irons goes wrong on him. I dont know how bad his irons will have to get before he will think they have went wrong on him but personly if I made some of the tee shots he made today I would certainly considder some kind of a change of weppons.

Mr Thomas is one of the kind of players that when it has took him more than 6 shots to get on the green he will turn to you and say how many have I had caddy and then you are suppose to pretend like you was thinking a minute and then say 4, then he will say to the man he is playing with well I did not know if I had shot 4 or 5 but the caddy says it is 4. You see in this way it is not him that is cheating but the caddy but he makes it up to the caddy afterwards with a $1.00 tip.

Mr Blake gives Mr Thomas a stroke a hole and they play a $10.00 nassua and niether one of them wins much money from the other one but even if they did why $10.00 is chickens food to men like they. But the way they crab and squak about different things you would think their last $1.00 was at stake. Mr Thomas started out this A. M. with a 8 and a 7 and of course that spoilt the day for him and me to. Theys lots of men that if they dont make a good score on the first 2 holes they will founder all the rest of the way around and raze H with their caddy and if I was laying out a golf course I would make the first 2 holes so darn easy that you could not help from getting a 4 or better on them and in that way everybody would start off good natured and it would be a few holes at lease before they begun to turn sour.

Mr Thomas was beat both in the A. M. and P. M. in spite of my help as Mr Blake is a pretty fair counter himself and I heard him say he got a 88 in the P. M. which is about a 94 but any way it was good enough to win. Mr Blakes regular game is about a 90 takeing his own figures and he is one of these cocky guys that takes his own game serious and snears at men that cant break 100 and if you was to ask him if he had ever been over 100 himself he would say not since the first yr he begun to play. Well I have watched a lot of those guys like he and I will tell you how they keep from going over 100 namely by doing just what he done this A. M. when he come to the 13th hole. Well he missed his tee shot and dubbed along and finely he got in a trap on his 4th shot and I seen him take 6 wallops in the trap and when he had took the 6th one his ball was worse off then when he started so he picked it up and marked a X down on his score card. Well if he had of played out the hole why the best he could of got was a 11 by holeing his next niblick shot but he would of probly got about a 20 which would of made him around 108 as he admitted takeing a 88 for the other 17 holes. But I bet if you was to ask him what score he had made he would say O I was terrible and I picked up on one hole but if I had of played them all out I guess I would of had about a 92.

These is the kind of men that laughs themselfs horse when they hear of some dub takeing 10 strokes for a hole but if they was made to play out every hole and mark down their real score their card would be decorated with many a big casino.

Well as I say I had a hard day and was pretty sore along towards the finish but still I had to laugh at Joe Bean on the 15th hole which is a par 3 and you can get there with a fair drive and personly I am genally hole high with a midiron, but Mr Thomas topped his tee shot and dubbed a couple with his mashie and was still quite a ways off the green and he stood studing the situation a minute and said to Mr Blake well I wonder what I better take here. So Joe Bean was standing by me and he said under his breath take my advice and quit you old rascal.

Mon. Apr. 17.

Yesterday was Sun and I was to wore out last night to write as I cadded 45 holes. I cadded for Mr Colby in the A. M. and Mr Langley in the P. M. Mr Thomas thinks golf is wrong on the sabath tho as Joe Bean says it is wrong any day the way he plays it.

This A. M. they was nobody on the course and I played 18 holes by myself and had a 5 for a 76 on the 18th hole but the wind got a hold of my drive and it went out of bounds. This P. M. they was 3 of us had a game of rummy started but Miss Rennie and Mrs Thomas come out to play and asked for me to caddy for them, they are both terrible.

Mrs Thomas is Mr Thomas wife and she is big and fat and shakes like jell and she always says she plays golf just to make her skinny and she dont care how rotten she plays as long as she is getting the exercise, well maybe so but when we find her ball in a bad lie she aint never sure it is hers till she picks it up and smells it and when she puts it back beleive me she don't cram it down no gopher hole.

Miss Rennie is a good looker and young and they say she is engaged to Chas Crane, he is one of our members and is the best player in the club and dont cheat hardly at all and he has got a job in the bank where Mr Thomas is the vice president. Well I have cadded for Miss Rennie when she was playing with Mr Crane and I have cadded for her when she was playing alone or with another lady and I often think if Mr

Crane could hear her talk when he was not around he would not be so stuck on her. You would be surprised at some of the words that falls from those fare lips.

Well the 2 ladies played for 2 bits a hole and Miss Rennie was haveing a terrible time wile Mrs Thomas was shot with luck on the greens and sunk 3 or 4 putts that was murder. Well Miss Rennie used some expressions which was best not repeated but towards the last the luck changed around and it was Miss Rennie that was sinking the long ones and when they got to the 18th tee Mrs Thomas was only 1 up.

Well we had started pretty late and when we left the 17th green Miss Rennie made the remark that we would have to hurry to get the last hole played, well it was her honor and she got the best drive she made all day about 120 yds down the fair way. Well Mrs Thomas got nervous and looked up and missed her ball a ft and then done the same thing right over and when she finely hit it she only knocked it about 20 yds and this made her lay 3. Well her 4th went wild and lit over in the rough in the apple trees. It was a cinch Miss Rennie would win the hole unless she dropped dead.

Well we all went over to hunt for Mrs Thomas ball but we would of been lucky to find it even in day light but now you could not hardly see under the trees, so Miss Rennie said drop another ball and we will not count no penalty. Well it is some job any time to make a woman give up hunting for a lost ball and all the more so when it is going to cost her 2 bits to play the hole out so there we stayed for at lease 10 minutes till it was so dark we could not see each other let alone a lost ball and finely Mrs Thomas said well it looks like we could not finish, how do we stand? Just like she did not know how they stood.

You had me one down up to this hole said Miss Rennie.

Well that is finishing pretty close said Mrs Thomas.

I will have to give Miss Rennie credit that what ever word she thought of for this occasion she did not say it out loud but when she was paying me she said I might of give you a quarter tip only I have to give Mrs Thomas a quarter she dont deserve so you dont get it.

Fat chance I would of had any way.

Thurs. Apr. 20.

Well we been haveing some more bad weather but today the weather was all right but that was the only thing that was all right. This P. M. I cadded double for Mr Thomas and Chas Crane the club champion who is stuck on Miss Rennie. It was a 4 some with he and Mr Thomas against Mr Blake and Jack Andrews the pro, they was only playing best ball so it was really just a match between Mr Crane and Jack Andrews and Mr Crane win by 1 up. Joe Bean cadded for Jack and Mr Blake. Mr Thomas was terrible and I put in a swell P. M. lugging that heavy bag of his besides Mr Cranes bag.

Mr Thomas did not go off of the course as much as usual but he kept hitting behind the ball and he run me ragged replaceing his divots but still I had to laugh when we was playing the 4th hole which you have to drive over a ravine and every time Mr Thomas misses his tee shot on this hole why he makes a squak about the ravine and says it ought not to be there and etc.

Today he had a terrible time getting over it and afterwards he said to Jack Andrews this is a joke hole and ought to be changed. So Joe Bean wispered to me that if Mr Thomas kept on playing like he was the whole course would be changed.

Then a little wile later when we come to the long 9th hole Mr Thomas got a fair tee shot but then he whiffed twice missing the ball by a ft and the 3d time he hit it but it only went a little ways and Joe Bean said that is 3 trys and no gain, he will have to punt.

But I must write down about my tough luck, well we finely got through the 18 holes and Mr Thomas reached down in his pocket for the money to pay me and he genally pays for Mr Crane to when they play together as Mr Crane is just a employ in the bank and dont have much money but this time all Mr Thomas had was a $20.00 bill so he said to Mr Crane I guess you will have to pay the boy Charley so Charley dug down and got the money to pay me and he paid just what it was and not a dime over, where if Mr Thomas had of had the change I would of got a $1.00 extra at lease and maybe I was not sore and Joe Bean to because of course Andrews never gives you nothing and Mr Blake dont tip his caddy unless he wins.

They are a fine bunch of tight wads said Joe and I said well Crane is all right only he just has not got no money.

He aint all right no more than the rest of them said Joe.

Well at lease he dont cheat on his score I said.

And you know why that is said Joe, neither does Jack Andrews cheat on his score but that is because they play to good. Players like Crane and Andrews that goes around in 80 or better cant cheat on their score because they make the most of the holes in around 4 strokes and the 4 strokes includes their tee shot and a couple of putts which everybody is right there to watch them when they make them and count them right along with them. So if they make a 4 and claim a 3 why people would just laugh in their face and say how did the ball get from the fair way on to the green, did it fly? But the boys that takes 7 and 8 strokes to a hole can shave their score and you know they are shaveing it but you have to let them get away with it because you cant prove nothing. But that is one of the penaltys for being a good player, you cant cheat.

To hear Joe tell it pretty near everybody are born crooks, well maybe he is right.

Wed. Apr. 26.

Today Mrs Doane was out for the first time this yr and asked for me to caddy for her and you bet I was on the job. Well how are you Dick she said, she always calls me by name. She asked me what had I been doing all winter and was I glad to see her and etc.

She said she had been down south all winter and played golf pretty near every day and would I watch her and notice how much she had improved.

Well to tell the truth she was no better then last yr and wont never be no better and I guess she is just to pretty to be a golf player but of course when she asked me did I think her game was improved I had to reply yes indeed as I would not hurt her feelings and she laughed like my reply pleased her. She played with Mr and Mrs Carter and I carried the 2 ladies bags wile Joe Bean cadded for Mr Carter. Mrs Carter is a ugly dame with things on her face and it must make Mr Carter feel sore when he looks at Mrs Doane to think he married Mrs Carter but I suppose they could not all marry the same one and besides Mrs Doane would not be a sucker enough to marry a man like he who drinks all the time and is pretty near always stood, tho Mr Doane who she did marry aint such a H of a man himself tho dirty with money.

They all gave me the laugh on the 3d hole when Mrs Doane was makeing her 2d shot and the ball was in the fair way but laid kind of bad and she just ticked it and then she asked me if winter rules was in force and I said yes so we teed her ball up so as she could get a good shot at it and they gave me the laugh for saying winter rules was in force.

You have got the caddys bribed Mr Carter said to her.

But she just smiled and put her hand on my sholder and said Dick is my pal. That is enough of a bribe to just have her touch you and I would caddy all day for her and never ask for a cent only to have her smile at me and call me her pal.

Sat. Apr. 29.

Today they had the first club tournament of the yr and they have a monthly tournament every month and today was the first one, it is a handicap tournament and everybody plays in it and they have prizes for low net score and low gross score and etc. I cadded for Mr Thomas today and will tell what happened.

They played a 4 some and besides Mr Thomas we had Mr Blake and Mr Carter and Mr Dunham. Mr Dunham is the worst man player in the club and the other men would not play with him a specialy on a Saturday only him and Mr Blake is partners together in business. Mr Dunham has got the highest handicap in the club which is 50 but it would have to be 150 for him to win a prize. Mr Blake and Mr Carter has got a handicap of about 15 a piece I think and Mr Thomas is 30, the first prize for the low net score for the day was a dozen golf balls and the second low score a ½ dozen golf balls and etc.

Well we had a great battle and Mr Colby ought to been along to write it up or some good writer. Mr Carter and Mr Dunham played partners against Mr Thomas and Mr Blake which ment that Mr Carter was playing Thomas and Blakes best ball, well Mr Dunham took the honor and the first ball he hit went strate off to the right and over the fence outside of the grounds, well he done the same thing 3 times. Well when he finely did hit one in the course why Mr Carter said why not let us not count them 3 first shots of Mr Dunham as they was practice. Like H we wont count them said Mr Thomas we must count every shot and keep our scores correct for the tournament.

All right said Mr Carter.

Well we got down to the green and Mr Dunham had about 11 and Mr Carter sunk a long putt for a par 5, Mr Blake all ready had 5 strokes and so did Mr Thomas and when Mr Carter sunk his putt why Mr Thomas picked his ball up and said Carter wins the hole and I and Blake will take 6s. Like H you will said Mr Carter, this is a tournament and we must play every hole out and keep our scores correct. So Mr Dunham putted and went down in 13 and Mr Blake got a 6 and Mr Thomas missed 2 easy putts and took a 8 and maybe he was not boiling.

Well it was still their honor and Mr Dunham had one of his dizzy spells on the 2d tee and he missed the ball twice before he hit it and then Mr Carter drove the green which is only a midiron shot and then Mr Thomas stepped up and missed the ball just like Mr Dunham. He was wild and yelled at Mr Dunham no man could play golf playing with a man like you, you would spoil anybodys game.

Your game was all ready spoiled said Mr Dunham, it turned sour on the 1st green.

You would turn anybody sour said Mr Thomas.

Well Mr Thomas finely took a 8 for the hole which is a par 3 and it certainly looked bad for him winning a prize when he started out with 2 8s, and he and Mr Dunham had another terrible time on No 3 and wile they was messing things up a 2 some come up behind us and hollered fore and we left them go through tho it was Mr Clayton and Mr Joyce and as Joe Bean said they was probly dissapointed when we left them go through as they are the kind that feels like the day is lost if they can write to some committee and preffer charges.

Well Mr Thomas got a 7 on the 3d and he said well it is no wonder I am off of my game today as I was up ½ the night with my teeth.

Well said Mr Carter if I had your money why on the night before a big tournament like this I would hire somebody else to set up with my teeth.

Well I wished I could remember all that was said and done but any way Mr Thomas kept getting sore and sore and we got to the 7th tee and he had not made a decent tee shot all day so Mr Blake said to him why dont you try the wood as you cant do no worse?

By Geo I beleive I will said Mr Thomas and took his driver out of the bag which he had not used it for 3 yrs.

Well he swang and zowie away went the ball pretty near 8 inchs distants wile the head of the club broke off clean and saled 50 yds down the course. Well I have got a hold on myself so as I dont never laugh out loud and I beleive the other men was scarred to laugh or he would of killed them so we all stood there in silents waiting for what would happen.

Well without saying a word he come to where I was standing and took his other 4 wood clubs out of the bag and took them to a tree which stands a little ways from the tee box and one by one he swang them with all his strength against the trunk of the tree and smashed them to H and gone, all right gentlemen that is over he said.

Well to cut it short Mr Thomas score for the first 9 was a even 60 and then we started out on the 2d 9 and you would not think it was the same man playing, on the first 3 holes he made 2 4s and a 5 and beat Mr Carter even and followed up with a 6 and a 5 and that is how he kept going up to the 17th hole.

What has got in to you Thomas said Mr Carter.

Nothing said Mr Thomas only I broke my hoodoo when I broke them 5 wood clubs.

Yes I said to myself and if you had broke them 5 wood clubs 3 yrs ago I would not of broke my back lugging them around.

Well we come to the 18th tee and Mr Thomas had a 39 which give him a 99 for 17 holes, well everybody drove off and as we was following along why Mr Klabor come walking down the course from the club house on his way to the 17th green to join some friends and Mr Thomas asked him what had he made and he said he had turned in a 93 but his handicap is only 12 so that give him a 81.

That wont get me no wheres he said as Charley Crane made a 75.

Well said Mr Thomas I can tie Crane for low net if I get a 6 on this hole.

Well it come his turn to make his 2d and zowie he hit the ball pretty good but they was a hook on it and away she went in to the woods on the left, the ball laid in behind a tree so as they was only one thing to do and that was waste a shot getting it back on the fair so that is what Mr Thomas done and it took him 2 more to reach the green.

How many have you had Thomas said Mr Carter when we was all on the green.

Let me see said Mr Thomas and then turned to me, how many have I had caddy?

I dont know I said.

Well it is either 4 or 5 said Mr Thomas.

I think it is 5 said Mr Carter.

I think it is 4 said Mr Thomas and turned to me again and said how many have I had caddy?

So I said 4.

Well said Mr Thomas personly I was not sure myself but my caddy says 4 and I guess he is right.

Well the other men looked at each other and I and Joe Bean looked at each other but Mr Thomas went ahead and putted and was down in 2 putts.

Well he said I certainly come to life on them last 9 holes.

So he turned in his score as 105 and with his handicap of 30 why that give him a net of 75 which was the same as Mr Crane so instead of Mr Crane getting 1 dozen golf balls and Mr Thomas getting ½ a dozen golf balls why they will split the 1st and 2d prize makeing 9 golf balls a piece.

Tues. May 2.

This was the first ladies day of the season and even Joe Bean had to carry for the fair sex. We cadded for a 4 some which was Miss Rennie and Mrs Thomas against Mrs Doane and Mrs Carter. I guess if they had of kept their score right the total for the 4 of them would of ran well over a 1000.

Our course has a great many trees and they seemed to have a traction for our 4 ladies today and we was in amongst the trees more then we was on the fair way.

Well said Joe Bean theys one thing about cadding for these dames, it keeps you out of the hot sun.

And another time he said he felt like a boy scout studing wood craft.

These dames is always up against a stump he said.

And another time he said that it was not fair to charge these dames regular ladies dues in the club as they hardly ever used the course.

Well it seems like they was a party in the village last night and of course the ladies was talking about it and Mrs Doane said what a lovely dress Miss Rennie wore to the party and Miss Rennie said she did not care for the dress herself.

Well said Mrs Doane if you want to get rid of it just hand it over to me.

I wont give it to you said Miss Rennie but I will sell it to you at ½ what it cost me and it was a bargain at that as it only cost me a $100.00 and I will sell it to you for $50.00.

I have not got $50.00 just now to spend said Mrs Doane and besides I dont know would it fit me.

Sure it would fit you said Miss Rennie, you and I are exactly the same size and figure, I tell you what I will do with you I will play you golf for it and if you beat me you can have the gown for nothing and if I beat you why you will give me $50.00 for it.

All right but if I loose you may have to wait for your money said Mrs Doane.

So this was on the 4th hole and they started from there to play for the dress and they was both terrible and worse then usual on acct of being nervous as this was the biggest stakes they had either of them ever played for tho the Doanes has got a bbl of money and $50.00 is chickens food.

Well we was on the 16th hole and Mrs Doane was 1 up and Miss Rennie sliced her tee shot off in the rough and Mrs Doane landed in some rough over on the left so they was clear across the course from each other. Well I and Mrs Doane went over to her ball and as luck would have it it had come to rest in a kind of a groove where a good player could not hardly make a good shot of it let alone Mrs Doane. Well Mrs Thomas was out in the middle of the course for once in her life and the other 2 ladies was over on the right side and Joe Bean with them so they was nobody near Mrs Doane and I.

Do I have to play it from there she said. I guess you do was my reply.

Why Dick have you went back on me she said and give me one of her looks.

Well I looked to see if the others was looking and then I kind of give the ball a shove with my toe and it come out of the groove and laid where she could get a swipe at it.

This was the 16th hole and Mrs Doane win it by 11 strokes to 10 and that made her 2 up and 2 to go. Miss Rennie win the 17th but they both took a 10 for the 18th and that give Mrs Doane the match.

Well I wont never have a chance to see her in Miss Rennies dress but if I did I aint sure that I would like it on her.

Fri. May 5.

Well I never thought we would have so much excitement in the club and so much to write down in my diary but I guess I better get busy writeing it down as here it is Friday and it was Wed. A. M. when the excitement broke loose and I was getting ready to play around when Harry Lear the caddy master come running out with the paper in his hand and showed it to me on the first page.

It told how Chas Crane our club champion had went south with $8000 which he had stole out of Mr Thomas bank and a swell looking dame that was a stenographer in the bank had elloped with him and they had her picture in the paper and I will say she is a pip but who would of thought a nice quiet young man like Mr Crane was going to prove himself a gay Romeo and a specialy as he was engaged to Miss Rennie tho she now says she broke their engagement a month ago but any way the whole affair has certainly give everybody something to talk about and one of the caddys Lou Crowell busted Fat Brunner in the nose because Fat claimed to of been the last one that cadded for Crane. Lou was really the last one and cadded for him last Sunday which was the last time Crane was at the club.

Well everybody was thinking how sore Mr Thomas would be and they would better not mention the affair around him and etc. but who should show up to play yesterday but Mr

Thomas himself and he played with Mr Blake and all they talked about the whole P. M. was Crane and what he had pulled.

Well Thomas said Mr Blake I am curious to know if the thing come as a surprise to you or if you ever had a hunch that he was libel to do a thing like this.

Well Blake said Mr Thomas I will admit that the whole thing come as a complete surprise to me as Crane was all most like my son you might say and I was going to see that he got along all right and that is what makes me sore is not only that he had proved himself dishonest but that he could be such a sucker as to give up a bright future for a sum of money like $8000 and a doll face girl that cant be no good or she would not of let him do it. When you think how young he was and the career he might of had why it certainly seems like he sold his soul pretty cheap.

That is what Mr Thomas had to say or at lease part of it as I cant remember a ½ of all he said but any way this P. M. I cadded for Mrs Thomas and Mrs Doane and that is all they talked about to, and Mrs Thomas talked along the same lines like her husband and said she had always thought Crane was to smart a young man to pull a thing like that and ruin his whole future.

He was getting $4000 a yr said Mrs Thomas and everybody liked him and said he was bound to get ahead so that is what makes it such a silly thing for him to of done, sell his soul for $8000 and a pretty face.

Yes indeed said Mrs Doane.

Well all the time I was listening to Mr Thomas and Mr Blake and Mrs Thomas and Mrs Doane why I was thinking about something which I wanted to say to them but it would of ment me looseing my job so I kept it to myself but I sprung it on my pal Joe Bean on the way home tonight.

Joe I said what do these people mean when they talk about Crane selling his soul?

Why you know what they mean said Joe, they mean that a person that does something dishonest for a bunch of money or a gal or any kind of a reward why the person that does it is selling his soul.

All right I said and it dont make no differents does it if the reward is big or little?

Why no said Joe only the bigger it is the less of a sucker the person is that goes after it.

Well I said here is Mr Thomas who is vice president of a big bank and worth a bbl of money and it is just a few days ago when he lied about his golf score in order so he would win 9 golf balls instead of a ½ a dozen.

Sure said Joe.

And how about his wife Mrs Thomas I said, who plays for 2 bits a hole and when her ball dont lie good why she picks it up and pretends to look at it to see if it is hers and then puts it back in a good lie where she can sock it.

And how about my friend Mrs Doane that made me move her ball out of a rut to help her beat Miss Rennie out of a party dress.

Well said Joe what of it?

Well I said it seems to me like these people have got a lot of nerve to pan Mr Crane and call him a sucker for doing what he done, it seems to me like $8000 and a swell dame is a pretty fair reward compared with what some of these other people sells their soul for, and I would like to tell them about it.

Well said Joe go ahead and tell them but maybe they will tell you something right back.

What will they tell me?

Well said Joe they might tell you this, that when Mr Thomas asks you how many shots he has had and you say 4 when you know he has had 5, why you are selling your soul for a $1.00 tip. And when you move Mrs Doanes ball out of a rut and give it a good lie, what are you selling your soul for? Just a smile.

O keep your mouth shut I said to him.

I am going to said Joe and would advice you to do the same.

12

A MEDIEVAL HOLE IN ONE

by Stephen Leacock

THE Canadian-born humourist Stephen Leacock has, if anything, written more comic stories on the topic of golf than
Ring Lardner. Like Lardner, he used his interest in the game
to create a series of now highly regarded tales such as 'The
Golfomaniac', 'The Golfer's Pocket Guide' and 'Tum and Play
Dolf', all of which are to be found in the numerous collections
of his prose. Leacock also wrote some amusing stories about
the way he imagined golf might be played in the future – and
how it could have been played in the past.

Perhaps the most ingenious of these little fantasies is 'A
Medieval Hole In One', first published in 1932. It is not only
Leacock at his funniest, but offers a most entertaining alterna-
tive explanation for one of the great moments of history . . .

A MEDIEVAL HOLE IN ONE

WET GOLF IN DRY HISTORY

The Middle Ages, from what we know about them, were days of pretty tall deeds and pretty tall talk. In the Middle Ages, if a man accomplished a feat of arms, or a feat of dexterity, or a feat of anything, he didn't let it get spoiled for want of telling. In witness of which take the marvellous accounts of archery, swordsmanship, strength, skill, and magic which fill the pages of medieval romance from the Chanson de Roland to Walter Scott.

And there is no doubt that the 'tall talk' of the Middle Ages was greatly helped along by the prevailing habit of tall drinking. They drank in those days not by the glass but by the barrel. They knew nothing of 'flasks' or 'cups' or 'glasses,' or such small degenerate measures as those of their descendants. When they wanted a real drink they knocked in the head of a 'cask' or 'tun' and gathered round it and drank it to the bottom of the barrel.

Even for a modest individual drink they needed a 'flagon' –

and a 'flagon' in the Middle Ages was of the same size as one of our garden watering-pots. A man who had inside him a couple of flagons of old 'Malmsey' or old 'Gascony,' had a power of talk and energy in him no longer known among us. When it is added that old 'Malmsey' only cost ten pennies for a full imperial gallon – six of our quarts – one can see that even the dark age had its bright spots and that history was not so dry as it is called.

As a result, not only were the deeds and feats of arms of the Middle Ages bigger than ours, but even the narration of them had more size. And the spectators and witnesses, having sopped up on their own account a few 'hogsheads' of 'mead' or sack, could see more, far more, than our poor dried-out audiences. In witness of which take any account of any tournament, bear-fight, bull-fight, archery match or rat-hunt anywhere from A.D. 1000 to 1500.

For all of which deeds and performances, the running accompaniment of knocking in hogsheads and draining flagons kept the whole event in character.

No king in the Middle Ages ever appeared at a public tournament or joust without ordering the ends of half a dozen casks of sack to be knocked in. No royal christening was ever held without 'tuns' of ale being distributed or 'broached' for the populace, and 'pipes' of wine being pumped into the nobility. At all big celebrations there were huge bonfires. Oxen were roasted whole. Any good man would get away with fifteen pounds of roast meat, six gallons of ale and a flagon of brandy, and go roaring home with an atmosphere round him like the mist round a brewery.

Those were great days. We cannot compete with them.

But in just one point the superiority is ours. The medieval people didn't have our opportunities. Their archery and their tournaments were poor stuff beside our games of today. Just think what would have happened if they had had such a thing as golf in the Middle Ages! Imagine the way in which, with their flagons of sack and their hogsheads of Malmsey right on the ground, they could have carried out a golf-match. Imagine what they could have done in the narration of it afterwards! Conceive what could have been made of a medieval Hole in One. Our poor unimaginative truth-telling generation can form but little idea as to how they would have dealt with it.

What follows below represents an account of a Hole in One, as achieved in the year A.D. 1215 and related after the style of medieval romance. It is based on the account of the famous tournament and meeting at Ashby de la Zouche (which is in England) during the reign of King John. On that famous occasion, as Walter Scott related in his *Ivanhoe*, there was an archery match between Hubert the Norman, the protégé of King John, and the Mysterious Bowman, Locksley, otherwise Robin Hood the Saxon Outlaw. In this contest Hubert 'sped his arrow' (that's the medieval name for what he did) with such consummate skill that it pierced the very centre of the bull's-eye, three hundred yards away. But Locksley had a still more consummate touch. He sped his shaft with such unerring dexterity that the point of it struck fair in the notch of Hubert's arrow, still sticking in the bull's-eye and split it into two exactly even halves! After which even the stingy King John had to treat the crowd, a whole meadowful, to about two firkins each.

Imagine what would happen if people who could write that kind of thing and people who could believe it had had a chance at a golf story.

Come! Let us turn Hubert and Locksley into their twentieth-century form and make the contest a Hole-in-One-Shot! Thus –

All was now prepared. The vast concourse of spectators, both Norman and Saxon, crowded the vacant spaces of the course, and even invaded the fairways from which the heralds and poursuivants sought in vain to dislodge them. The humbler churls, or jarls, clustered in the branches of the trees.

At intervals along the course great 'butts' or 'tuns', by which we mean 'vats,' had been placed, from which not only the yeomanry but even the commonry were permitted that day to drink at the King's expense.

King John was seated on a dais beside the sand-box of Tee

No. 1, at the edge of which the pious Archbishop Stephen Langton knelt in prayer for the success of the Norman Hubert. Around and about the tee, on tiers of rudely contrived benches, the Knights of the Household in full (autumn) armour were mingled with the resplendent Ladies of the Court.

'Sirrah!' said the King, turning sternly to Hubert, 'dost think thou canst outswat this Saxon fellow?'

'My grandsire,' said Hubert, 'played in the Hastings handicap, and it shall go hard with me an I fall short of his score.'

The King scowled but said nothing.

'What is bogey?' whispered Roger Bigod, Earl of Bygod, to Sir John Montfaucon de la Tour, who stood beside him near the tee.

'Three, so it thinks me,' answered Sir John.

'And gives either of the contestants as it were a bisque or holeth he in one stroke the fewer?'

'Nay,' said Montfaucon, 'they play as man to man, or as who should say at scratch.'

At this moment the loud sound of a tucket armoured by the winding of a hobo from the second tee announced that the lists were clear.

'Let the course be measured!' commanded the Chief Marshal.

On this Sir Roger Mauleverer of the Tower and Sir Eustace, the Left-handed, Constable of the Cowstable, attended by six poursuivants carrying a line of silken yarn, measured the distance.

'How stands it?' asked the King.

'Four hundred ells, six firkins, and a demilitre,' answered the Marshal.

At the mention of this distance – which corresponds in our modern English to more than four hundred yards – an intense hush fell upon the attendant crowd. That a mere ball no larger than a pheasant's egg could be driven over this tremendous distance by a mere blow from a mere wand of hickory, daunted the mere imagination.

The King, who well knew that the approaching contest was in reality one between Norman and Saxon and might carry with it the loss of his English crown, could ill conceal the fears that racked his evil conscience. In vain his cup-bearer fetched him goblet after goblet of Gascony. Even the generous wine failed to enliven the mind or to dissipate the fears of the doomed monarch. A great silence had fallen upon the assembled knights and ladies, broken only by the murmured prayers of the saintly archbishop kneeling beside the sand-box. Even the stout hearts of such men as Sir Roger Bigod de Bygod and Sir Walter de la Tenspot almost ceased to beat.

'Have done with this delay,' exclaimed the King. 'Let the men begin.'

Hubert the Norman stepped first on to the tee. His lithe frame, knit to a nicety, with every bone and joint working to its full efficiency, was encased in a jerkin of Andalusian wool, over a haut-de-chausse, or plus eight, of quilted worsted. He carried in his right hand a small white ball, while in his left he bore a shaft or club of hickory, the handle bound with cordovan leather and the end, or tip, or as the Normans called it, the *bout*, fashioned in a heavy knob flattened on one side to a hexagonal diagonal.

The manner of the Norman Hubert was grave, but his firm movements and his steady eye showed no trace of apprehension as he adjusted the ball upon a small heap of sand upon the forward, or front, part of the tee.

'Canst do it?' queried the agonizing King, his hands writhing nervously on the handle of his sceptre.

'My grandsire . . .' began Hubert.

'You said that before,' cried John. 'Shoot!'

Hubert bowed and paused a moment to drink a flagon of Amsterdam gin handed to him by the King's boutellier, or bottle-washer. Then, standing poised on the balls of his feet at a distance of two Norman demis (twenty-six and a half English inches) from the ball, he waved his club in the air as if testing its weight, while his keen eye measured the velocity of the wind.

Then, as the crowd waited in breathless silence, Hubert suddenly swung the hickory to his full reach behind his shoulder and brought it down in a magnificent sweep, striking the ball with its full impact.

There was a loud resilient 'click,' distinctly heard by the

spectators at the second tee, while a great shout arose from all the Normans as the ball rose in the air describing a magnificent parabola in its flight.

'A Hubert! A Hubert!' they shouted. *'Par le Sang de Dieu,'* exclaimed Sir Roger Bigod de Bygod, 'some stroke!'

Meantime the ball, glistening in the sunshine and seeming to gather force in its flight, swept above the fairway and passed high in the air over the ground-posts that marked the hundred, the two hundred, and the three hundred ells, still rushing to its goal.

'By the body of St Augustine!' cried the pious Guillaume de la Hootch, ''twill reach the green itself!'

'It has!' shouted Sir Roger Bigod. 'Look! Look! They are seizing and lifting the flag! 'Tis on! 'Tis in! By the shirt of St Ambrose, the ball is in the can!'

And as Sir Roger spoke a great shout went up from all the crowd, echoed even by the Saxon churls who lined the branches of the trees. 'A Hole in One! A Hole in One!' cried the multitude, while an immediate rush was made to the barrels or vats of mead which lined the course, into which the exultant populace precipitated themselves head first.

For such readers as do not understand the old Norman game of Goffe, or Gouffe – sometimes also called Guff – it is proper to explain that in the centre of each *parterre* or *terrace*, sometimes called a *Green* or *Pelouse* – it was customary to set a sunken receptacle or can, of the kind used by the Normans to can tomatoes, into which the ball must ultimately be driven. The virtue of Hubert's stroke was that he had driven the ball into the can (a feat for which many Normans required eight, ten, or even twenty strokes) in one single blow, an achievement called in old Norman a 'Hole in One.'

And now the voice of the Chief Herald could be heard calling through hautboy or megaphone:

'Hole No. 1; stroke No. 1. Hubert of Normandy scores Hole in One. Player in hand, J. Locksley, of Huntingdon, England. Clear the fairway for shot No. 2.'

All eyes now turned to where the splendid figure of the mysterious Locksley, the Unknown Golfer or Gopher, ascended the first tee. It was known to all that this was in reality none other, or little other, than the Saxon outlaw Robin Hood, who was whispered to be the Earl of Huntingdon and half whispered to be, by his descent from his own grandmother, the Saxon claimant to the throne.

'How now, Locksley!' sneered the triumphant John as the Saxon appeared beside him, 'canst beat that?'

Every gaze rested upon Locksley as he stood leaning upon his hickory club. His mysterious appearance at Ashby de la Zouche and the whispers as to his identity lent to him a romantic, and almost fearsome interest, while his magnificent person marked him as the beau-ideal of the Saxon Golfer still seen at times even in the mimic contests of to-day.

His powerful form could have touched the balance at two hundred and eighty-five pounds avoirdupois. The massive shoulders would have seemed out of proportion but for the ample sweep of the girth or waistline and the splendid breadth of the netherward or rearward hindquarters.

He was clad, like Hubert, in woollen jerkin and plus eights, and he bore on his feet the terrific spiked sandals of the Saxon, capable of inflicting a mortal blow.

Locksley placed his ball, and then, grasping in his iron grip the leather-bound club-headed hickory hexagonal, he looked about him with complete sang-froid and even something of amusement.

The King's boozelier, or booze-hound, now approached Locksley and, after the courtesy of the age, offered him a horn, or 'jolt' of gin. The Saxon put it aside and to the astonishment of the crowd called only for water, contenting himself with a single bucketful.

'Drink'st not?' said the scowling King.

'Not in hours of busyness,' said Locksley firmly.

'And canst thou outdo Hubert's shot?' sneered John.

'I know not,' said Locksley carelessly; 'Hubert's shot was not half bad, but I'll see if I can touch up his ball for him in the tomato can.'

'Have done with boasting!' cried the King. 'Tell the archbishop to count three, and then let the fellow shoot. If he fail, my lord Montfaucon and you, Roger Bigod of Bygod, see that he does not leave the tee alive.'

The archbishop raised his saintly face towards the skies and began to count.

'Unum!' he said, using the neuter gender of the numeral adjective in accordance with the increasing deterioration of the Latin language which had already gone far in the year A.D. 1215.

'Duo,' said the archbishop, and then in a breathless hush, as the word 'tres' quivered on the lips of the ecclesiastic, Locksley's club cleft the air in a single flash of glittering sunlight and descended upon the ball with such force that the sound of the concussion echoed back from the woods beyond the farthest green.

In a moment the glittering trajectory of the missile could be followed high in its flight and then the curve of its rushing descent towards the green. For a moment the silence was so intense that even the faint rustling of the grass was audible to the ear, then the crashing concussion of the driven ball against the inner tin of the tomato can showed that Locksley also had achieved a Hole in One! But the gasp or gulp of astonishment had hardly passed when the crowd became aware that Locksley's skilled marksmanship had far surpassed the feat of a Hole in One accomplished by his opponent. His ball, driven with a power and accuracy that might wellnigh seem incredible, had struck against Hubert's ball inside the can at exactly the angle necessary to drive it out with great force and start it back in flight towards the first tee.

To the amazement of all beholders, Hubert's ball, easily distinguishable by two little dots on its lower face, was seen rushing in rapid flight to retrace its course above the fairway. So true was its path that it landed back precisely on the tee from which Hubert had shot it and came to rest on the little pile of sand on which the Norman gopher had originally placed it.

'By God!' shouted Bigod of Bygod, as Locksley picked up the ball and handed it with a bow to King John.

A wild shout that rose alike from the Saxon Thanes, the Danes, and even the Normans, rent the air, while even the ladies of the court, carried away in a burst of chivalrous admiration, tore off their silken baldrics and threw them at the feet of the victor.

Nobles and commons alike, Norman and Saxon together seized axe or bill and began beating in the heads of the casks in their eagerness to drink the health of the victor.

'A Locksley! A Locksley!' cried the multitude. For the moment the King paused. His ear caught in the roaring plaudits of the crowd the first note of that mighty unison of Saxon and Norman voices which was destined to cast him from his power.

He knew that any attempt against the life or person of the Saxon chieftain was without avail.

He turned to the venerable archbishop, who was prostrate beside the tee, eating sand.

'Fetch me the Magna Carta,' he said, 'and I'll sign it.'

13

WARTIME GOLF

by George C. Nash

P_{UNCH} magazine played an invaluable role in keeping its readers' spirits up during the years of the Second World War by its irreverent humour directed against the Nazis and the Fascists. It helped to foster an attitude that regardless of the tyrannical dictators of Germany and Italy, the British spirit *would* survive – as would its heritage and most cherished activities, such as golf. Indeed, many a determined golfer still managed to get in a round or two when other duties were not pressing, and despite the actions of enemy bombers many courses remained intact and playable – though often not without considerable ingenuity on the part of those entrusted with keeping them open.

During these war years, *Punch* readers who enjoyed golfing humour got a regular tonic from a series entitled, 'Letters to the Secretary of a Golf Club', written by one of the magazine's regular contributors and an enthusiast of the game, George C. Nash. These missives humorously described a concern with the game that quite overshadowed the larger problems of the war itself! The episode that I have selected as typifying the series as a whole concerns the worry of one member that enemy parachutists could use the golf course as a landing point, and thereby damage the precious turf! It appeared in the issue of June 12, 1940.

WARTIME GOLF

LETTERS TO THE SECRETARY OF A GOLF CLUB

From Richard Singleton, Club Member, Roughover Golf Club.

DEAR MR SECRETARY, – Are you aware that when the Germans invaded Holland a great many parachutists were dropped on the golf courses there?

Choice of this particular type of country was deliberate and made for obvious reasons –

(*a*) Excellent cover afforded.

(*b*) Improbability of meeting with human elements – especially military.

(c) No telephone-wires, houses or church spires to impede descent.

I suppose you have been asleep (as usual) to the possibilities of their doing the same thing at Roughover.

For heaven's sake wake up.

Yours faithfully,

R. SINGLETON.

PS. – Regarding *cover* (see (*a*) above), one of the first things you ought to do is to fill up all the *deeper* bunkers. As you are well aware, I have for years advocated this (though for other reasons!) especially at the 14th, 'Satan's Gullet,' and at the 3rd, 'Grant's Cavern.' Both of these hazards would make admirable places for the concealment of at least a couple of score of the enemy.

From Admiral Charles Sneyring-Stymie, C.B., R.N. (Retd.), The Bents, Roughover. (Chairman Green Committee.)

DEAR WHELK, – Singleton has been at me about the Germans landing on the links. He is quite right. You *must* take immediate action. Better have all the fairways wired and strewn with impediments; also get the bell at the blind 17th manned by a wideawake squad of caddies so that instant alarm of an impending descent may be given. (Ten sharp clangs with the bell's clapper every thirty seconds ought to do for 'public warning' and one clang every ten seconds for 'all clear' or 'raiders passed'.)

I hear Lionel Nutmeg (Malayan Civil Service Retd.) is getting his old elephant gun ready. If you can have this piece of information confirmed, and in the interests of the public's safety, I think you ought to warn the police that he is expected to be at large at any moment.

Yours faithfully,

C. SNEYRING-STYMIE.

From General Sir Armstrong Forcursue, K.B.E., C.S.I.(late Indian Army Retd.), The Cedars, Roughover. (By hand.)

MY DEAR WHELK, – This parachute business can be solved as easily as falling off a log, and believe me, the whole affair only requires a little imagination – and I have got THE VERY THING.

I was talking to Carstairs of the General Outfitters Co, Ltd, in the High Street this morning and he asked me if three old plaster models (Sportsmen's Mannequin Series) complete with lifelike face and adjustable limbs would be of any use to the coming War Supplies Depot's Jumble Sale. Of course when he first mentioned them I asked the man what on earth he took me for; but I have since seen the possibility of their being put to the greatest national use and have just telephoned him to have them left round here at the house as soon as possible.

And now for the plan, which is simplicity itself – *just to dress up the plaster models in some of my old army uniforms and place them in various elevated positions about the links where they can be readily seen from the air.* Reaction on the enemy is obvious, but as you're always so bone dense I'd better explain that the mere fact of three army officers being on duty like *that* will be bound to deter anyone who might be thinking of 'dropping off.'

So far as our own club members are concerned (and those few of the public who find their way on to the links) I feel quite sure that once they know what the models are there for, and once they get used to them, the whole thing will soon cease to attract attention. I'm afraid, however, that poor old Crookshanks will almost certainly complain that they put him off his game, but you must just be firm with him and tell him there is a war on and he must stretch a point.

As I cannot get the models into position entirely by myself, please come and lend me a hand to dress them up and carry them out on to the course.

Yours sincerely,
ARMSTRONG FORCURSUE.

PS. – To show you how little imagination people have got over this parachute scare – just fancy, that fool Warburtin has bought up every bull-terrier he can lay his hands on in the country. He is training them to go for anything human on sight, with the result that only yesterday one of them took a great hunk out of his wife's shin while she was weeding her herbaceous border. If you ask me, it serves him damn well right.

PPS. – Better come round immediately on receipt of this. Have dinner with us – we can get busy afterwards and put the things out before dusk.

From Mrs Plantain (wife of Mr Plantain, Greenkeeper, Roughover Golf Club). (By Hand.)

SIR, – Please Sir, for goodness sake to come quick for the husband has just taken to his bed owing to what he saw on going out to work at 7 a.m. this morning. And Sir, it is those German parrychooters and they is here all right in our midst, and no mistake, for the husband saw three of them dressed up in old-fashioned British Army uniforms and standing there indifferent like and as if they did not wish to call attention to theirselves. This, he says, was proved by the way one of them was pointing a pair of field-glasses at a clump of whins, another acting he was playing golf, and the third kidding on he was fishing.

Well Sir, for a time the husband just looked his fill, like a rabbit at a weasel and with his heart in his throat, and then Sir he nearly jumped right out of his skin; for suddenly there was a great rushing wind and a lot of swear words just behind him and immediately later there was three loud explosions, and Sir, a moment later *still* the parrychooters was all stone dead.

And it was *that there* club member, Mr Nutmeg, what is always scowling at everyone, that had bagged the lot – and he did it with the big dangerous gun that he threatened the new groundsman with for not raking the bunkers last summer.

But Sir, what made the husband run home here with the hair on him standing straight up and his lips blue and wanting to blow his nose and to get in quickly under the blankets was *this* – that when the last invader fell over he saw as plain as plain a lot of sawdust and blue smoke and bits of china come out of the dead man's stomach. And, Sir, it was enough to terrify the bravest in the land you must allow.

[149]

Well, Mr Whelk, that is the absolute gospel, for the husband has touched no liquor since the last budget and only a drop then on account of the war-time price, and he is not the one to tell any lies except when provoked by members. So please Sir come quick and bring a doctor with you for he is still sweating something cronic, and I am feared he is in a bad way.

Your obedient Servt,
ANNIE PLANTAIN

From General Sir Armstrong Forcursue, K.B.E., C.S.I., The Cedars, Roughover. (By Hand.)

DEAR WHELK, – Your report received and I have already told the police to have Nutmeg arrested immediately. It is a clear case of sabotage.

Yours faithfully,
ARMSTRONG FORCURSUE.

PS. – Ever since I caught him out telling me he had played eight instead of nine in the 1934 October Club Medal I knew he could never be trusted again. It is amazing we have nursed such a viper in our bosom for so long.

14

AN UNLUCKY GOLFER

by A. A. Milne

A. A. MILNE, the poet, playwright and creator of the indefatigable Winnie the Pooh, was also a contributor to the pages of *Punch* as well as being a golfing enthusiast. He played the game resolutely, but never managed to get his handicap below double figures and was typically rather deprecating of his ability in conversation and in print.

Milne was a great believer that games – any games – should be played seriously but not taken *too* seriously. He always looked for the humour in sport, and some of his essays on cricket and rugby – two of his other interests – are among the funniest items to be found in collections such as *By Way of Introduction* (1929) and *The Day's Play* (1949). As far as golf is concerned, he was at his very best when writing this next item, 'An Unlucky Golfer'. Anyone who has ever played golf has his own little disaster story to tell, but the narrator seems to have endured a catalogue of mishaps with unfailing good humour.

AN UNLUCKY GOLFER

I am the world's unluckiest golfer.

Yes, I know what you are going to say, but I don't mean what you mean. Of the ordinary bad luck which comes to us all at times I do not complain. It is the 'rub of the green'. When my best drive is caught by cover, or fielded smartly by mid-on with his foot; when I elect to run a bunker ten yards away and am most unfortunately held up by blown sand (or, as I generally call it, dashed sand); when I arrive at last on the green, and my only hope of winning the hole is that my opponent shall pick up a worm which he ought to have brushed away, or brush away one which he ought to have picked up ... and there are no worms out this morning; on all these occasions I take my ill-luck with a shrug of the shoulders and something as nearly like a smile as I can manage. After all, golf would be a very dull game if it were entirely a matter of skill.

It is in another way altogether that I am singled out by Fate. Once I have driven off the first tee, she is no more unkind to me than to the others. By that time she has done her worst. But sometimes it is as much as I can do to get on to the first tee at all, so relentless is her persecution of me. Surely no other golfer is so obstructed.

I suppose my real trouble is that I take golf too seriously. When I arranged many years ago to be at St Margaret's at 2.30 on Wednesday, I *was* at St Margaret's at 2.30 on Wednesday. I didn't ring up suddenly and say that I had a cold, or that my dog wanted a run, or that a set of proofs had just arrived which had to be corrected quickly. No, I told myself that an engagement was an engagement. '*Wednesday, St Margaret's, 2.30*' – I turned up, and have never regretted it. If to-day my appointment is '*Sunningdale, Thursday, 10.45*', it is as certain that I shall be there. But these other golfers, one wonders how they ever get married at all.

I am not saying that they are careless about their promises; not all of them; but that, in their case, the mere fact of making an important appointment seems to bring out something: spots or a jury-summons or a new baby. I suppose that, when they play with each other, they hardly notice these obstructions, for if A has to plead an unexpected christening on the Monday, B practically knows that he will have to have his tonsils removed suddenly on the Thursday, when the return match is to be played; wherefore neither feels resentment against the other. Only I, who take golf seriously, am surprised. 'Tonsils, juries, christenings,' I say to myself, 'but I thought we were playing *golf.*'

But not only am I a serious golfer, I am, as I have said, the world's unluckiest one. The most amazing things happen to the people who arrange to play with me. On the very morning of our game they are arrested for murder, summoned to Buckingham Palace, removed to asylums, sent disguised to Tibet, or asked to play the leading part in *Hamlet* at twenty-four hours' notice. Any actor out of work would be wise to fix up a game with me, for on that day he would almost certainly be sent for to start rehearsing. Of course he might have a fatal accident instead, but that is a risk which he would have to take.

However, it is time that you saw my golf in action. Here, then, is a typical day, unexaggerated.

On a certain Wednesday I was to play a couple of rounds with a friend. On Tuesday afternoon I rang him up on the telephone to remind him of our engagement, and in the course of a little talk before we hung our receivers up, I said that I had just been lunching with an actor-manager, and he said that he had just been bitten by a mosquito. Not that it mattered to the other in the least, but one must have one's twopennyworth.

Wednesday dawned, as it has a habit of doing, but never did it dawn so beautifully as now; the beginning of one of those lovely days of early autumn than which nothing is more lovely. That I was to spend the whole of this beautiful day playing golf, not working, was almost too good to be believed. I sang as I climbed into my knickerbockers; I was still singing as I arranged the tassels of my garters . . . And, as I went down to breakfast, the telephone bell began to sing.

I knew at once, of course. With all the experience I have had, I knew. I merely wondered whether it was the man himself who was dead, or one of his friends.

'Hallo!' said his voice. So he was alive.

'Yes?' I said coldly.

'Hallo! I say, you remember the mosquito?' (*Which mosquito?*) 'Well, my leg is about three times its ordinary size.' (*Does that matter? I thought. None of us is really symmetrical.*) 'I can hardly move it . . . Doctor . . . Nurses . . . Amputate . . . In bed for a year . . .' He babbled on, but I was not listening. I was wondering if I could possibly find somebody else. It is a funny thing, but somehow I cannot write in knickerbockers. Once I have put them on, I find it impossible to work. I *must* play golf. But alas! how difficult to find another at such short notice. As a last hope I decided to ring up Z. Z is almost as keen a golfer as myself. No such trifle as a lack of uniformity in his legs would keep *him* from his game. I cut off the other fellow as he was getting to the middle of his third operation, and got on to Z. Z, thank Heaven for him, would play.

I called for him. We drove down. We arrived. With each succeeding minute the morning became more lovely; with each succeeding minute I thanked Heaven more for Z. As we walked over to the caddie-master I was almost crying with

happiness. Never was there day more beautiful. All this mosquito business had made us late, and there were no caddies
left, but did I mind? Not a bit! On a morning like this, I
thought to myself as I stepped on to the first tee, I couldn't
mind anything.

The moment that Z stepped on to the first tee, I knew that I
was mistaken. You will never believe it, but I give you my
word that it is true. Z stepped on to the wrong bit of the first
tee, uttered one loud yell . . . and collapsed on the grass with a
broken ankle . . .

You say that I might have left him there and played a few
holes by myself? I did. But it was necessary to give instruc-
tions for him to be removed before others came after me. I
forget the exact rule about loose bodies on the tee, but a fussy
player might easily have objected. So I had to go back and tell
the secretary, and one way and another I was delayed a good
deal. And of course it spoiled my day entirely.

But I was not surprised. As I say, I am the world's unluckiest
golfer.

15

THOSE IN PERIL ON THE TEE

by P. G. Wodehouse

ALTHOUGH there are a considerable number of people who believe that the funniest character to be found in golfing literature is P. G. Wodehouse's 'Oldest Member', there are others who maintain that the stories of Mr Mulliner and his encounters with the golfing fraternity are even more amusing. I happen to belong to the latter group, which is why I have selected one of that imperturbable gentleman's hilarious yarns for this collection. That, and the fact that the 'Oldest Member' stories are all easily obtainable in a single volume, *The Golf Omnibus*.

Wodehouse, who has rightly been declared one of the greatest humorous writers of our times, was a life-long golf enthusiast, though as he wrote in 1973 when he had reached the remarkable age of 92, 'I was never much of a golfer . . . I was always one of the dregs, the sort of man whose tee shots, designed to go due north, invariably went nor-nor-east or in a westerly direction. But *how* I loved the game!' And just to underline the fact, the great writer added, 'If only I had taken up golf earlier and devoted my whole time to it instead of fooling about writing stories and things, I might have got my handicap down to under eighteen!' Of course, if P. G. had been as good as his word we readers would not be able to enjoy one of the richest and funniest treasure troves of golfing stories from a single pen.

Picking the best of Wodehouse's golf stories is, of course, impossible for they are all good and just about every one has someone to champion it. So I will just add that 'Those In Peril On The Tee' still makes me chuckle after repeated readings, and amply supports this verdict given on the Mr Mulliner stories a few years back, 'He is one of P. G. Wodehouse's funniest creations – nothing can dull his sunny outlook on life ... and nothing will stop him telling an uproarious tale when he wants to.' So please read on ...

THOSE IN PERIL ON THE TEE

I think the two young men in the chessboard knickerbockers were a little surprised when they looked up and perceived Mr Mulliner brooding over their table like an affable Slave of the Lamp. Absorbed in their conversation, they had not noticed his approach. It was their first visit to the Anglers' Rest, and their first meeting with the Sage of its bar-parlour: and they were not yet aware that to Mr Mulliner any assemblage of his fellow-men over and above the number of one constitutes an audience.

'Good evening, gentlemen,' said Mr Mulliner. 'You have been playing golf, I see.'

They said they had.

'You enjoy the game?'

They said they did.

'Perhaps you will allow me to request Miss Postlethwaite, princess of barmaids, to re-fill your glasses?'

They said they would.

'Golf,' said Mr Mulliner, drawing up a chair and sinking smoothly into it, 'is a game which I myself have not played for some years. I was always an indifferent performer, and I gradually gave it up for the simpler and more straightforward pastime of fishing. It is a curious fact that, gifted though the Mulliners have been in virtually every branch of life and sport, few of us have ever taken kindly to golf. Indeed, the only member of the family I can think of who attained to any real proficiency with the clubs was the daughter of a distant cousin of mine – one of the Devonshire Mulliners who married a man named Flack. Agnes was the girl's name. Perhaps you have run across her? She is always playing in tournaments and competitions, I believe.'

The young men said No, they didn't seem to know the name.

'Ah?' said Mr Mulliner. 'A pity. It would have made the story more interesting to you.'

The two young men exchanged glances.

'Story?' said the one in the slightly more prismatic knicker-bockers, speaking in a voice that betrayed agitation.

'Story?' said his companion, blenching a little.

'The story,' said Mr Mulliner, 'of John Gooch, Frederick Pilcher, Sidney McMurdo and Agnes Flack.'

The first young man said he didn't know it was so late. The second young man said it was extraordinary how time went. They began to talk confusedly about trains.

'The story,' repeated Mr Mulliner, holding them with the effortless ease which makes this sort of thing such child's play to him, 'of Agnes Flack, Sidney McMurdo, Frederick Pilcher and John Gooch.'

It is an odd thing (said Mr Mulliner) how often one finds that those who practise the Arts are quiet, timid little men, shy in company and unable to express themselves except through the medium of the pencil or the pen. I have noticed it again and again. John Gooch was like that. So was Frederick Pilcher. Gooch was a writer and Pilcher was an artist, and they used to meet a good deal at Agnes Flack's house, where they were constant callers. And every time they met John Gooch would say to himself, as he watched Pilcher balancing a cup of tea and smiling his weak, propitiatory smile, 'I am fond of Frederick, but his best friend could not deny that he is a pretty dumb brick.' And Pilcher, as he saw Gooch sitting on the edge of his chair and fingering his tie, would reflect, 'Nice fellow as John is, he is certainly a total loss in mixed society.'

Mark you, if ever men had an excuse for being ill at ease in the presence of the opposite sex, these two had. They were both eighteen-handicap men, and Agnes was exuberantly and dynamically scratch. Her physique was an asset to her, especially at the long game. She stood about five feet ten in her stockings, and had shoulders and forearms which would have excited the envious admiration of one of those muscular women on the music-halls, who good-naturedly allow six brothers, three sisters, and a cousin by marriage to pile themselves on her collarbone while the orchestra plays a long-drawn chord and the audience hurries out to the bar. Her eye resembled the eye of one of the more imperious queens of history: and when she laughed, strong men clutched at their temples to keep the tops of their heads from breaking loose.

Even Sidney McMurdo was as a piece of damp blotting-paper in her presence. And he was a man who weighed two hundred and eleven pounds and had once been a semi-finalist in the Amateur Championship. He loved Agnes Flack with an ox-like devotion. And yet – and this will show you what life is – when she laughed, it was nearly always at him. I am told by those in a position to know that, on the occasion when he first proposed to her – on the sixth green – distant rumblings of her mirth were plainly heard in the club-house locker-room, causing two men who were afraid of thunderstorms to scratch their match.

Such, then, was Agnes Flack. Such, also, was Sidney McMurdo. And such were Frederick Pilcher and John Gooch.

Now John Gooch, though, of course, they had exchanged a word from time to time, was in no sense an intimate of Sidney McMurdo. It was consequently a surprise to him when one night, as he sat polishing up the rough draft of a detective story – for his was the talent that found expression largely in blood, shots in the night, and millionaires who are found murdered in locked rooms with no possible means of access except a window forty feet above the ground – the vast bulk of McMurdo lumbered across his threshold and deposited itself in a chair.

The chair creaked. Gooch stared. McMurdo groaned.

'Are you ill?' said John Gooch.

'Ha!' said Sidney McMurdo.

He had been sitting with his face buried in his hands, but now he looked up; and there was a red glare in his eyes which sent a thrill of horror through John Gooch. The visitor reminded him of the Human Gorilla in his novel, *The Mystery of the Severed Ear*.

'For two pins,' said Sidney McMurdo, displaying a more mercenary spirit than the Human Gorilla, who had required no cash payment for his crimes, 'I would tear you into shreds.'

'Me?' said John Gooch, blankly.

'Yes, you. And that fellow Pilcher, too.' He rose; and, striding to the mantelpiece, broke off a corner of it and crumbled it in his fingers. 'You have stolen her from me.'

'Stolen? Whom?'

'My Agnes.'

John Gooch stared at him, thoroughly bewildered. The idea of stealing Agnes Flack was rather like the notion of sneaking off with the Albert Hall. He could make nothing of it.

'She is going to marry you.'

'What!' cried John Gooch, aghast.

'Either you or Pilcher.' McMurdo paused. 'Shall I tear you into little strips and tread you into the carpet?' he murmured, meditatively.

'No,' said John Gooch. His mind was blurred, but he was clear on that point.

'Why did you come butting in?' groaned Sidney McMurdo, absently taking up the poker and tying it into a lover's knot. 'I was getting along splendidly until you two pimples broke out. Slowly but surely I was teaching her to love me, and now it can never be. I have a message for you. From her. I proposed to her for the eleventh time tonight; and when she had finished laughing she told me that she could never marry a mere mass of brawn. She said she wanted brain. And she told me to tell you and the pest Pilcher that she had watched you closely and realised that you both loved her, but were too shy to speak, and that she understood and would marry one of you.'

There was a long silence.

'Pilcher is a splendid fellow,' said John Gooch. 'She must marry Pilcher.'

'She will, if he wins the match.'

'What match?'

'The golf match. She read a story in a magazine the other day where two men played a match at golf to decide which was to win the heroine; and about a week later she read another story in another magazine where two men played a match at golf to decide which was to win the heroine. And a couple of days ago she read three more stories in three more magazines where exactly the same thing happened; and she has decided to accept it as an omen. So you and the hound Pilcher are to play eighteen holes, and the winner marries Agnes.'

'The winner?'

'Certainly.'

'I should have thought – I forget what I was going to say.'

McMurdo eyed him keenly.

'Gooch,' he said, 'You are not one of those thoughtless butterflies, I hope, who go about breaking girls' hearts?'

'No, no,' said John Gooch, learning for the first time that this was what butterflies did.

'You are not one of those men who win a good girl's love and then ride away with a light laugh?'

John Gooch said he certainly was not. He would not dream of laughing, even lightly, at any girl. Besides, he added, he could not ride. He had once had three lessons in the Park, but had not seemed to be able to get the knack.

'So much the better for you,' said Sidney McMurdo heavily. 'Because, if I thought that, I should know what steps to take. Even now . . .' He paused, and looked at the poker in a rather yearning sort of way. 'No, no,' he said, with a sigh, 'better not, better not.' He flung the thing down with a gesture of resignation. 'Better, perhaps, on the whole not.' He rose, frowning.

'Well, good night, weed,' he said. 'The match will be played on Friday morning. And may the better – or, rather, the less impossibly foul – man win.'

He banged the door, and John Gooch was alone.

But not for long. Scarcely half an hour had passed when the door opened once more to admit Frederick Pilcher. The artist's face was pale, and he was breathing heavily. He sat down, and after a brief interval contrived to summon up a smile. He rose and patted John Gooch on the shoulder.

'John,' he said, 'I am a man who as a general rule hides his feelings. I mask my affections. But I want to say, straight out, here and now, that I like you, John.'

'Yes?' said John Gooch.

Frederick Pilcher patted his other shoulder.

'I like you so much, John, old man, that I can read your thoughts, strive to conceal them though you may. I have been watching you closely of late, John, and I know your secret. You love Agnes Flack.'

'I don't!'

'Yes, you do. Ah, John, John,' said Frederick Pilcher, with a gentle smile, 'why try to deceive an old friend? You love her, John. You love that girl. And I have good news for you, John – tidings of great joy. I happen to know that she will look favourably on your suit. Go in and win, my boy, go in and win. Take my advice and dash round and propose without a moment's delay.'

John Gooch shook his head. He, too, smiled a gentle smile.

'Frederick,' he said, 'this is like you. Noble. That's what I call it. Noble. It's the sort of thing the hero does in act two. But it must not be, Frederick. It must not, shall not be. I also can read a friend's heart, and I know that you, too, love Agnes Flack. And I yield my claim. I am excessively fond of you, Frederick, and I give her up to you. God bless you, old fellow. God, in fact, bless both of you.'

'Look here,' said Frederick Pilcher, 'have you been having a visit from Sidney McMurdo?'

'He did drop in for a minute.'

There was a tense pause.

'What I can't understand,' said Frederick Pilcher, at length, peevishly, 'is why, if you don't love this infernal girl, you kept calling at her house practically every night and sitting goggling at her with obvious devotion.'

'It wasn't devotion.'

'It looked like it.'

'Well, it wasn't. And, if it comes to that, why did you call on her practically every night and goggle just as much as I did?'

'I had a very good reason,' said Frederick Pilcher. 'I was studying her face. I am planning a series of humorous drawings on the lines of Felix the Cat, and I wanted her as a model. To goggle at a girl in the interests of one's Art, as I did, is a very different thing from goggling wantonly at her, like you.'

'Is that so?' said John Gooch. 'Well, let me tell you that I wasn't goggling wantonly. I was studying her psychology for a series of stories which I am preparing, entitled *Madeline Monk, Murderess*.'

Frederick Pilcher held out his hand.

'I wronged you, John,' he said. 'However, be that as it may, the point is that we both appear to be up against it very hard. An extraordinarily well-developed man, that fellow McMurdo.'

'A mass of muscle.'

'And of a violent disposition.'

'Dangerously so.'

Frederick Pilcher drew out his handkerchief and dabbed at his forehead.

'You don't think, John, that you might ultimately come to love Agnes Flack?'

'I do not.'

'Love frequently comes after marriage, I believe.'

'So does suicide.'

'Then it looks to me,' said Frederick Pilcher, 'as if one of us is for it. I see no way out of playing that match.'

'Nor I.'

'The growing tendency on the part of the modern girl to read trashy magazine stories,' said Frederick Pilcher severely, 'is one that I deplore. I view it with alarm. And I wish to goodness that you authors wouldn't write tales about men who play golf matches for the hand of a woman.'

'Authors must live,' said John Gooch. 'How is your game these days, Frederick?'

'Improved, unfortunately. I am putting better.'

'I am steadier off the tee.' John Gooch laughed bitterly. 'When I think of the hours of practice I have put in, little knowing that a thing of this sort was in store for me, I appreciate the irony of life. If I had not bought Sandy McHoots' book last spring I might now be in a position to be beaten five and four.'

'Instead of which, you will probably win the match on the twelfth.'

John Gooch started.

'You can't be as bad as that!'

'I shall be on Friday.'

'You mean to say you aren't going to try?'

'I do.'

'You have sunk to such depths that you would deliberately play below your proper form?'

'I have.'

'Pilcher,' said John Gooch, coldly, 'you are a hound, and I never liked you from the start.'

You would have thought that, after the conversation which I have just related, no depth of low cunning on the part of Frederick Pilcher would have had the power to surprise John Gooch. And yet, as he saw the other come out of the clubhouse to join him on the first tee on the Friday morning, I am not exaggerating when I say that he was stunned.

John Gooch had arrived at the links early, wishing to get in a little practice. One of his outstanding defects as a golfer was a pronounced slice; and it seemed to him that, if he drove off a few balls before the match began, he might be able to analyse this slice and see just what was the best stance to take up in order that it might have full scope. He was teeing his third ball when Frederick Pilcher appeared.

'What – what – what —!' gasped John Gooch.

For Frederick Pilcher, discarding the baggy, mustard-coloured plus-fours in which it was his usual custom to infest the links, was dressed in a perfectly-fitting morning-coat, yellow waistcoat, striped trousers, spats, and patent-leather shoes. He wore a high stiff collar, and on his head was the glossiest top-hat ever seen off the Stock Exchange. He looked intensely uncomfortable; and yet there was on his face a smirk which he made no attempt to conceal.

'What's the matter?' he asked.

'Why are you dressed like that?' John Gooch uttered an exclamation. 'I see it all. You think it will put you off your game.'

'Some idea of the kind did occur to me,' replied Frederick Pilcher, airily.

'You fiend!'

'Tut, tut, John. These are hard words to use to a friend.'

'You are no friend of mine.'

'A pity,' said Frederick Pilcher, 'for I was hoping that you would ask me to be your best man at the wedding.' He took a club from his bag and swung it. 'Amazing what a difference clothes make. You would hardly believe how this coat cramps the shoulders. I feel as if I were a sardine trying to wriggle in its tin.'

The world seemed to swim before John Gooch's eyes. Then the mist cleared, and he fixed Frederick Pilcher with a hypnotic gaze.

'You are going to play well,' he said, speaking very slowly and distinctly. 'You are going to play well. You are going to play well. You ——'

'Stop it!' cried Frederick Pilcher.

'You are going to play well. You are going ——'

A heavy hand descended on his shoulder. Sidney McMurdo was regarding him with a black scowl.

'We don't want any of your confounded chivalry,' said Sidney McMurdo. 'This match is going to be played in the strictest spirit of —— What the devil are you dressed like that for?' he demanded, wheeling on Frederick Pilcher.

'I – I have to go into the City immediately after the match,' said Pilcher. 'I sha'n't have time to change.'

'H'm. Well, it's your own affair. Come along,' said Sidney McMurdo, gritting his teeth. 'I've been told to referee this match, and I don't want to stay here all day. Toss for the honour, worms.'

John Gooch spun a coin. Frederick Pilcher called tails. The coin fell heads up.

'Drive off, reptile,' said Sidney McMurdo.

As John Gooch addressed his ball, he was aware of a strange sensation which he could not immediately analyse. It was only when, after waggling two or three times, he started to draw his club back that it flashed upon him that this strange sensation was confidence. For the first time in his life he seemed to have no doubt that the ball, well and truly struck, would travel sweetly down the middle of the fairway. And then the hideous truth dawned on him. His subconscious self had totally misunderstood the purport of his recent remarks and had got the whole thing nicely muddled up.

Much has been written of the subconscious self, and all that has been written goes to show that of all the thick-headed, blundering chumps who take everything they hear literally, it is the worst. Anybody of any intelligence would have realised that when John Gooch said, 'You are going to play well,' he was speaking to Frederick Pilcher; but his subconscious self had missed the point completely. It had heard John Gooch say, 'You are going to play well,' and it was seeing that he did so.

The unfortunate man did what he could. Realising what had happened, he tried with a despairing jerk to throw his swing out of gear just as the club came above his shoulder. It was a fatal move. You may recall that when Arnaud Massy won the British Open Championship one of the features of his play was a sort of wiggly twiggle at the top of the swing, which seemed to have the effect of adding yards to his drive. This wiggly twiggle John Gooch, in his effort to wreck his shot, achieved to a nicety. The ball soared over the bunker in which he had hoped to waste at least three strokes; and fell so near the green that it was plain that only a miracle could save him from getting a four.

There was a sardonic smile on Frederick Pilcher's face as he stepped on to the tee. In a few moments he would be one down, and it would not be his fault if he failed to maintain the advantage. He drew back the head of his club. His coat, cut by a fashionable tailor who, like all fashionable tailors, resented it if the clothes he made permitted his customers to breathe, was so tight that he could not get the club-head more than half-way up. He brought it to this point, then brought it down in a lifeless semi-circle.

'Nice!' said Sidney McMurdo, involuntarily. He despised and disliked Frederick Pilcher, but he was a golfer. And a golfer cannot refrain from giving a good shot its meed of praise.

For the ball, instead of trickling down the hill as Frederick Pilcher had expected, was singing through the air like a shell. It fell near John Gooch's ball and, bounding past it, ran on to the green.

The explanation was, of course, simple. Frederick Pilcher was a man who, in his normal golfing costume, habitually overswung. This fault the tightness of his coat had now rendered impossible. And his other pet failing, the raising of the head, had been checked by the fact that he was wearing a top-hat. It had been Pilcher's intention to jerk his head till his spine cracked; but the unseen influence of generations of ancestors who had devoted the whole of their intellect to the balancing of top-hats on windy days was too much for him.

A minute later the two men had halved the hole in four.

The next hole, the water-hole, they halved in three. The third, long and over the hill, they halved in five.

And it was as they moved to the fourth tee that a sort of madness came upon both Frederick Pilcher and John Gooch simultaneously.

These two, you must remember, were eighteen-handicap men. That is to say, they thought well of themselves if they could get sixes on the first, sevens on the third, and anything from fours to elevens on the second – according to the number of balls they sank in the water. And they had done these three holes in twelve. John Gooch looked at Frederick Pilcher and Frederick Pilcher looked at John Gooch. Their eyes were gleaming, and they breathed a little stertorously through their noses.

'Pretty work,' said John Gooch.

'Nice stuff,' said Frederick Pilcher.

'Get a move on, blisters,' growled Sidney McMurdo.

It was at this point that the madness came upon these two men.

Picture to yourself their position. Each felt that by continuing to play in this form he was running a deadly risk of having to marry Agnes Flack. Each felt that his opponent could not possibly keep up so hot a pace much longer, and the prudent course, therefore, was for himself to ease off a bit before the crash came. And each, though fully aware of all this, felt that he was dashed if he wasn't going to have a stab at doing the round of his life. It might well be that having started off at such a clip, he would find himself finishing somewhere in the eighties. And that, surely, would compensate for everything.

After all, felt John Gooch, suppose he did marry Agnes Flack, what of it? He had faith in his star, and it seemed to him that she might quite easily get run over by a truck or fall off a cliff during the honeymoon. Besides, with all the facilities for divorce which modern civilisation so beneficently provides, what was there to be afraid of in marriage, even with an Agnes Flack?

Frederick Pilcher's thoughts were equally optimistic. Agnes Flack, he reflected, was undeniably a pot of poison; but so much the better. Just the wife to keep an artist up to the mark. Hitherto he had had a tendency to be a little lazy. He had avoided his studio and loafed about the house. Married to Agnes Flack, his studio would see a lot more of him. He would spend all day in it – probably have a truckle bed put in and never leave it at all. A sensible man, felt Frederick Pilcher, can always make a success of marriage if he goes about it in the right spirit.

John Gooch's eyes gleamed. Frederick Pilcher's jaw protruded. And neck and neck, fighting grimly for their sixes and sometimes even achieving fives, they came to the ninth green, halved the hole, and were all square at the turn.

It was at this point that they perceived Agnes Flack standing on the club-house terrace.

'Yoo-hoo!' cried Agnes in a voice of thunder.

And John Gooch and Frederick Pilcher stopped dead in

their tracks, blinking like abruptly-awakened somnambulists.

She made a singularly impressive picture, standing there with her tweed-clad form outlined against the white of the club-house wall. She had the appearance of one who is about to play Boadicea in a pageant; and John Gooch, as he gazed at her, was conscious of a chill that ran right down his back and oozed out at the soles of his feet.

'How's the match coming along?' she yelled, cheerily.

'All square,' replied Sidney McMurdo, with a sullen scowl. 'Wait where you are for a minute, germs,' he said. 'I wish to have a word with Miss Flack.'

He drew Agnes aside and began to speak to her in a low rumbling voice. And presently it was made apparent to all within a radius of half a mile that he had been proposing to her once again, for suddenly she threw her head back and there went reverberating over the countryside that old familiar laugh.

'Ha, ha, ha, ha, ha, ha, HA!' laughed Agnes Flack.

John Gooch shot a glance at his opponent. The artist, pale to the lips, was removing his coat and hat and handing them to his caddie. And, even as John Gooch looked, he unfastened his braces and tied them round his waist. It was plain that from now on Frederick Pilcher intended to run no risk of not overswinging.

John Gooch could appreciate his feelings. The thought of how that laugh would sound across the bacon and eggs on a rainy Monday morning turned the marrow in his spine to ice and curdled every red corpuscle in his veins. Gone was the exhilarating ferment which had caused him to skip like a young ram when a long putt had given him a forty-six for the first nine. How bitterly he regretted now those raking drives, those crisp flicks of the mashie-niblick of which he had been so proud ten minutes ago. If only he had not played such an infernally good game going out, he reflected, he might at this moment be eight or nine down and without a care in the world.

A shadow fell between him and the sun; and he turned to see Sidney McMurdo standing by his side, glaring with a singular intensity.

'Bah!' said Sidney McMurdo, having regarded him in silence for some moments.

He turned on his heel and made for the club-house.

'Where are you going, Sidney?' asked Agnes Flack.

'I am going home,' replied Sidney McMurdo, 'before I murder these two miserable harvest-bugs. I am only flesh and blood, and the temptation to grind them into powder and scatter them to the four winds will shortly become too strong. Good morning.'

Agnes emitted another laugh like a steam-riveter at work.

'Isn't he funny?' she said, addressing John Gooch, who had clutched at his scalp and was holding it down as the vibrations died away. 'Well, I suppose I shall have to referee the rest of the match myself. Whose honour? Yours? Then drive off and let's get at it.'

The demoralising effects of his form on the first nine holes had not completely left John Gooch. He drove long and straight, and stepped back appalled. Only a similar blunder on the part of his opponent could undo the damage.

But Frederick Pilcher had his wits well about him. He overswung as he had never overswung before. His ball shot off into the long grass on the right of the course, and he uttered a pleased cry.

'Lost ball, I fancy,' he said. 'Too bad!'

'I marked it,' said John Gooch, grimly. 'I will come and help you find it.'

'Don't trouble.'

'It is no trouble.'

'But it's your hole, anyway. It will take me three or four to get out of there.'

'It will take me four or five to get a yard from where I am.'

'Gooch,' said Frederick Pilcher, in tones equally hushed, 'you are a low bounder. And if I find you kicking that ball under a bush, there will be blood shed – and in large quantities.'

'Ha, ha!'

'Ha, ha to you!' said John Gooch.

The ball was lying in a leathery tuft, and, as Pilcher had

predicted, it took three strokes to move it back to the fairway. By the time Frederick Pilcher had reached the spot where John Gooch's drive had finished, he had played seven.

But there was good stuff in John Gooch. It is often in times of great peril that the artistic temperament shows up best. Missing the ball altogether with his next three swings, he topped it with his fourth, topped it again with his fifth, and, playing the like, sent a low, skimming shot well over the green into the bunker beyond. Frederick Pilcher, aiming for the same bunker, sliced and landed on the green. The six strokes which it took John Gooch to get out of the sand decided the issue. Frederick Pilcher was one up at the tenth.

But John Gooch's advantage was shortlived. On the right, as you approach the eleventh green there is a deep chasm, spanned by a wooden bridge. Frederick Pilcher, playing twelve, just failed to put his ball into this, and it rolled on to within a few feet of the hole. It seemed to John Gooch that the day was his. An easy mashie-shot would take him well into the chasm, from which no eighteen-handicap player had ever emerged within the memory of man. This would put him two down – a winning lead. He swung jubilantly, and brought off a nicely-lofted shot which seemed to be making for the very centre of the pit.

And so, indeed, it was; and it was this fact that undid John Gooch's schemes. The ball, with all the rest of the chasm to choose from, capriciously decided to strike the one spot on the left-hand rail of the wooden bridge which would deflect it towards the flag. It bounded high in the air, fell on the green, and the next moment, while John Gooch stood watching with fallen jaw and starting eyes, it had trickled into the hole.

There was a throbbing silence. Then Agnes Flack spoke.

'Important, if true,' she said. 'All square again. I will say one thing for you two – you make this game very interesting.'

And once more she sent the birds shooting out of the tree-tops with that hearty laugh of hers. John Gooch, coming slowly to after the shattering impact of it, found that he was clutching Frederick Pilcher's arm. He flung it from him as if it had been a loathsome snake.

A grimmer struggle than that which took place over the next

six holes has probably never been seen on any links. First one, then the other seemed to be about to lose the hole, but always a well-judged slice or a timely top enabled his opponent to rally. At the eighteenth tee the game was still square; and John Gooch, taking advantage of the fact that Agnes had stopped to tie her shoe-lace, endeavoured to appeal to his one-time friend's better nature.

'Frederick,' he said, 'this is not like you.'

'What isn't like me?'

'Playing this low-down game. It is not like the old Frederick Pilcher.'

'Well, what sort of a game do you think you are playing?'

'A little below my usual, it is true,' admitted John Gooch. 'But that is due to nervousness. You are deliberately trying to foozle, which is not only painting the lily but very dishonest. And I can't see what motive you have, either.'

'You can't, can't you?'

John Gooch laid a hand persuasively on the other's shoulder.

'Agnes Flack is a most delightful girl.'

'Who is?'

'Agnes Flack.'

'A delightful girl?'

'Most delightful.'

'Agnes Flack is a delightful girl?'

'Yes.'

'Oh?'

'She would make you very happy.'

'Who would?'

'Agnes Flack.'

'Make me happy?'

'Very happy.'

'Agnes Flack would make me happy?'

'Yes.'

'Oh?'

John Gooch was conscious of a slight discouragement. He did not seem to be making headway.

'Well, then, look here,' he said, 'what we had better do is to have a gentleman's agreement.'

'Who are the gentlemen?'

'You and I.'

'Oh?'

John Gooch did not like the other's manner, nor did he like the tone of voice in which he had spoken. But then there were so many things about Frederick Pilcher that he did not like that it seemed useless to try to do anything about it. Moreover, Agnes Flack had finished tying her shoe-lace, and was making for them across the turf like a mastodon striding over some prehistoric plain. It was no time for wasting words.

'A gentleman's agreement to halve the match,' he said hurriedly.

'What's the good of that? She would only make us play extra holes.'

'We would halve those, too.'

'Then we should have to play it off another day.'

'But before that we could leave the neighbourhood.'

'Sidney McMurdo would follow us to the ends of the earth.'

'Ah, but suppose we didn't go there? Suppose we simply lay low in the city and grew beards?'

'There's something in it,' said Frederick Pilcher, reflectively.

'You agree?'

'Very well.'

'Splendid!'

'What's splendid?' asked Agnes Flack, thudding up.

'Oh – er – the match,' said John Gooch. 'I was saying to Pilcher that this was a splendid match.'

Agnes Flack sniffed. She seemed quieter than she had been at the outset, as though something were on her mind.

'I'm glad you think so,' she said. 'Do you two always play like this?'

'Oh, yes. Yes. This is about our usual form.'

'H'm! Well, push on.'

It was with a light heart that John Gooch addressed his ball for the last drive of the match. A great weight had been lifted from his mind, and he told himself that now there was no objection to bringing off a real sweet one. He swung lustily; and the ball, struck on its extreme left side, shot off at right angles, hit the ladies' tee-box, and, whizzing back at a high rate of speed, would have mown Agnes Flack's ankles from under her, had she not at the psychological moment skipped in a manner extraordinarily reminiscent of the high hills mentioned in Sacred Writ.

'Sorry, old man,' said John Gooch, hastily, flushing as he encountered Frederick Pilcher's cold look of suspicion. 'Frightfully sorry, Frederick, old man. Absolutely unintentional.'

'What are you apologising to *him* for?' demanded Agnes Flack with a good deal of heat. It had been a near thing, and the girl was ruffled.

Frederick Pilcher's suspicions had plainly not been allayed by John Gooch's words. He drove a cautious thirty yards, and waited with the air of one suspending judgment for his opponent to play his second. It was with a feeling of relief that John Gooch, smiting vigorously with his brassie, was enabled to establish his *bona fides* with a shot that rolled to within mashie-niblick distance of the green.

Frederick Pilcher seemed satisfied that all was well. He played his second to the edge of the green. John Gooch ran his third up into the neighbourhood of the pin.

Frederick Pilcher stooped and picked his ball up.

'Here!' cried Agnes Flack.

'Hey!' ejaculated John Gooch.

'What on earth do you think you're doing?' said Agnes Flack.

Frederick Pilcher looked at them with mild surprise.

'What's the matter?' he said. 'There's a blob of mud on my ball. I just wanted to brush it off.'

'Oh, my heavens!' thundered Agnes Flack. 'Haven't you ever read the rules? You're disqualified.'

'Disqualified?'

'Dis-jolly-well-qualified,' said Agnes Flack, her eyes flashing scorn. 'This cripple here wins the match.'

Frederick Pilcher heaved a sigh.

'So be it,' he said. 'So be it.'

'What do you mean, so be it? Of course it is.'

'Exactly. Exactly. I quite understand. I have lost the match. So be it.'

And, with drooping shoulders, Frederick Pilcher shuffled off in the direction of the bar.

John Gooch watched him go with a seething fury which for the moment robbed him of speech. He might, he told himself, have expected something like this. Frederick Pilcher, lost to every sense of good feeling and fair play, had double-crossed him. He shuddered as he realised how inky must be the hue of Frederick Pilcher's soul; and he wished in a frenzy of regret that he had thought of picking his own ball up. Too late! Too late!

For an instant the world had been blotted out for John Gooch by a sort of red mist. This mist clearing, he now saw Agnes Flack standing looking at him in a speculative sort of way, an odd expression in her eyes. And beyond her, leaning darkly against the club-house wall, his bulging muscles swelling beneath his coat and his powerful fingers tearing to pieces what appeared to be a section of lead piping, stood Sidney McMurdo.

John Gooch did not hesitate. Although McMurdo was some distance away, he could see him quite clearly; and with equal clearness he could remember every detail of that recent interview with him. He drew a step nearer to Agnes Flack, and having gulped once or twice, began to speak.

'Agnes,' he said huskily, 'there is something I want to say to you. Oh, Agnes, have you not guessed ——'

'One moment,' said Agnes Flack. If you're trying to propose to me, sign off. There is nothing doing. The idea is all wet.'

'All wet?'

'All absolutely wet. I admit that there was a time when I toyed with the idea of marrying a man with brains, but there are limits. I wouldn't marry a man who played golf as badly as you do if he were the last man in the world. Sid-nee!' she roared, turning and cupping her mouth with her hands; and a nervous golfer down by the lake-hole leaped three feet and got his mashie entangled between his legs.

'Hullo?'

'I'm going to marry you, after all.'

'Me?'

'Yes, you.'

'Three rousing cheers!' bellowed McMurdo.

Agnes Flack turned to John Gooch. There was something like commiseration in her eyes, for she was a woman. Rather on the large side, but still a woman.

'I'm sorry,' she said.

'Don't mention it,' said John Gooch.

'I hope this won't ruin your life.'

'No, no.'

'You still have your Art.'

'Yes, I still have my Art.'

'Are you working on anything just now?' asked Agnes Flack.

'I'm starting a new story tonight,' said John Gooch. 'It will be called *Saved From the Scaffold*.'

16

IS A GOLFER A GENTLEMAN?

by A. P. Herbert

Sɪʀ Aʟᴀɴ Hᴇʀʙᴇʀᴛ's stories about Mr Albert Haddock and his seemingly endless series of disputes with the letter of the law are also regarded as among the classic humorous tales of the twentieth century. Sir Alan, who first studied for the bar but gave up the profession to become a writer, was an infrequent golfer and only played with literary friends from either the stage or from publishing circles. One of his partners was the playwright, Nigel Playfair, with whom he collaborated on his first theatrical success, *Riverside Nights*, in 1926. However, golfing topics did surface in some of his essays for *Punch* as well as in collections of his articles now to be found in books such as *What a Word* (1935).

A. P. Herbert campaigned for much of his life against jargon and 'officialese', and it was through the mouth of Albert Haddock that he fired some of his most stinging barbs. In the following case of Rex *v.* Haddock, the language of a sorely pressed golfer – i.e. Mr Haddock – is the subject of a prosecution which will undoubtedly strike a chord with any golfer who has ever found his temper under stress from the vagaries of the game . . .

REX *v.* HADDOCK

IS A GOLFER A GENTLEMAN?

(*Before the Stipendiary*)

This case, which raised an interesting point of law upon the meaning of the word 'gentleman', was concluded today.

The *Stipendiary*, giving judgment, said: In this case the defendant, Mr Albert Haddock, is charged under the Profane Oaths Act, 1745, with swearing and cursing on a Cornish golf course. The penalty under the Act is a fine of one shilling for every day-labourer, soldier, or seaman, two shillings for every other person under the degree of gentleman, and five shillings for every person of or above the degree of gentleman – a remarkable but not unfortunately unique example of a statute which lays down one law for the rich and another (more lenient) for the poor. The fine, it is clear, is leviable not upon the string or succession of oaths, but upon each individual malediction (see *Reg.* v. *Scott* (1863), 33 L.J.M. 15). The curses charged, and admitted, in this case, are over four hundred in number, and we are asked by the prosecution to inflict a fine of one hundred pounds, assessed on the highest or gentleman's rate at five shillings a swear. The defendant admits the offences, but contends that the fine is excessive and wrongly calculated, on the curious ground that he is not a gentleman when he is playing golf.

He has reminded us in a brilliant argument that the law takes notice, in many cases, of such exceptional circumstances as will break down the normal restraints of a civilised citizen and so powerfully inflame his passions that it would be unjust and idle to apply to his conduct the ordinary standards of the law; as, for example, where without warning or preparation he discovers another man in the act of molesting his wife or family. Under such provocation the law recognises that a reasonable man ceases for the time being to be a reasonable man; and the defendant maintains that in the special circumstances of his offence a gentleman ceases to be gentleman and should not be judged or punished as such.

Now, what were these circumstances? Broadly speaking, they were the 12th hole on the Mullion golf course, with which most of us in the Court are familiar. At that hole the player drives (or does not drive) over an inlet of the sea which is enclosed by cliffs some sixty feet high. The defendant has told us that he never drives over, but always into, this inlet, or Chasm, as it is locally named. A steady but not sensational player on other sections of the course, before this obstacle his normal powers invariably desert him. This, he tells us, has preyed upon his mind; he has registered, it appears, a kind of vow, and year after year, at Easter and in August, he returns to this county determined ultimately to overcome the Chasm.

Meanwhile, unfortunately, his tenacity has become notorious. It is the normal procedure, it appears, if a ball is struck into the Chasm, to strike a second, and, if that should have no better fate, to abandon the hole. The defendant tells us that in the past he has struck no fewer than six or seven balls in this way, some rolling gently over the cliff and some flying far and high out to sea. But recently, grown fatalistic, he has not thought it worth while to make even a second attempt, but has immediately followed his first ball into the Chasm, and there, among the rocks, small stones, and shingle, has hacked at his ball with the appropriate instrument until some lucky blow has lofted it on to the turf above, or, in the alternative, until he has broken his instruments or suffered some injury from flying fragments of rock. On one or two occasions a crowd of holiday-makers and local residents have gathered on the cliff and foreshore to watch the defendant's indomitable struggles and to hear the verbal observations which have accompanied them. On the date of the alleged offences a crowd of unprecedented dimensions collected, but so intense was the defendant's concentration that he did not, he tells us, notice their presence. His ball had more nearly traversed the gulf than ever before; it struck the opposing cliff but a few feet from the summit, and nothing but an adverse gale of exceptional ferocity prevented success. The defendant therefore, as he conducted his customary excavations among the boulders of the Chasm, was possessed, he tells us, by a more than customary fury. Oblivious of his surroundings, conscious only of the will to win, for fifteen or twenty minutes he lashed his battered ball against the stubborn cliffs, until at last it triumphantly escaped. And before, during, and after every stroke he uttered a number of imprecations of a complex character which were carefully recorded by an assiduous caddie and by one or two of the spectators. The defendant says that he recalls with shame a few of the expressions which he used, that he has never used them before, and that it was a shock to him to hear them issuing from his own lips; and he says quite frankly that no gentleman would use such language.

Now this ingenious defence, whatever may be its legal value, has at least some support in the facts of human experience. I am a golf-player myself – (*laughter*) – but, apart from

[182]

that, evidence has been called to show the subversive effect of this exercise upon the ethical and moral systems of the mildest of mankind. Elderly gentlemen, gentle in all respects, kind to animals, beloved by children, and fond of music, are found in lonely corners of the downs, hacking at sand-pits or tussocks of grass, and muttering in a blind, ungovernable fury elaborate maledictions which could not be extracted from them by robbery or murder. Men who would face torture without a word become blasphemous at the short fourteenth. And it is clear that the game of golf may well be included in that category of intolerable provocations which may legally excuse or mitigate behaviour which is not otherwise excusable, and that under that provocation the reasonable or gentle man may reasonably act like a lunatic or lout respectively, and should legally be judged as such.

But then I have to ask myself, What does the Act intend by the words 'of or above the degree of gentleman'? Does it intend a fixed social rank or a general habit of behaviour? In other words, is a gentleman legally always a gentleman, as a duke or solicitor remains unalterably a duke or solicitor? For if this is the case the defendant's argument must fail. The prosecution says that the word 'degree' is used in the sense of 'rank'. Mr Haddock argues that it is used in the sense of an university examination, and that, like the examiners, the Legislature divides the human race, for the purposes of swearing, into three vague intellectual or moral categories, of which they give certain rough but not infallible examples. Many a first-class man has taken a third, and many a day-labourer, according to Mr Haddock, is of so high a character that under the Act he should rightly be included in the first 'degree'. There is certainly abundant judicial and literary authority for the view that by 'gentleman' we mean a personal quality and not a social status. We have all heard of 'Nature's gentlemen'. 'Clothes do not make the gentleman,' said Lord Mildew in Cook v. The Mersey Docks and Harbour Board (1896), 2 A.C., meaning that a true gentleman might be clad in the foul rags of an author. In the old maxim 'Manners makyth man' (See Charles v. The Great Western Railway) there is no dubt that by 'man' is meant 'gentleman', and that 'manners' is contrasted with wealth or station. Mr Thomas, for the prosecution, has quoted against these authorities an observation of the poet Shakespeare that:

> The Prince of Darkness is a gentleman,

but quotations from Shakespeare are generally meaningless and always unsound. This one, in my judgment, is both. I am more impressed by the saying of another author (whose name I forget) that the King can make a nobleman, but he cannot make a gentleman.

I am satisfied therefore that the argument of the defendant has substance. Just as the reasonable man who discovers his consort in the embraces of the supplanter becomes for the moment a raving maniac, so the habitually gentle man may become in a bunker a violent, unmannerly oaf. In each case the ordinary sanctions of the law are suspended; and while it is right that a normally gentle person should in normal circumstances suffer a heavier penalty for needless imprecations than a common seaman or cattle-driver, for whom they are part of the tools of his trade, he must not be judged by the standards of the gentle in such special circumstances as provoked the defendant.

That provocation was so exceptional that I cannot think it was contemplated by the framers of the Act; and had golf at that date been a popular exercise I have no doubt that it would have been dealt with under a special section. I find therefore that this case is not governed by the Act. I find that the defendant at the time was not in law responsible for his actions or his speech and I am unable to punish him in any way. For his conduct in the Chasm he will be formally convicted of Attempted Suicide while Temporarily Insane, but he leaves the court without a stain upon his character. (*Applause*).

17

THE TEMPTATION OF ADMIRAL JUDDY

by Ben Travers

BEN TRAVERS is the master of the light farce whose plays have been an integral part of the theatre scene for half a century and more. Not a few of these, such as *A Cuckoo in the Nest* (1925), have also been filmed. The best known of Travers' farces have been regularly revived – the most recent of these being *Rookery Nook* which was first put on at the Aldwych Theatre in London in 1926 and then restaged in 1987!

Cricket was actually Ben Travers' first sporting love, but he occasionally enjoyed a round of golf with friends and, according to some of these, was capable of being a low handicap player. Like so many of the other contributors to this book, he was a keen observer of the foibles of those who played the game with something akin to obsession, and 'The Temptation of Admiral Juddy' is a hilarious send up of just such a person. It also happens to be as funny a story as any he wrote for the stage or his novels. Any feminist perusing these pages will probably enjoy the Admiral's come-uppance as a result of his attitude towards women golfers, too!

THE TEMPTATION OF ADMIRAL JUDDY

Few gentlemen with a record more remarkable than that of Mr Ruby can ever have bestowed their patronage upon the comparatively insignificant town of Chumpton-on-Sea. Yet he arrived there unheralded and unsung. The town band made no effort to turn out in his honour. For him no glad banners kissed the breeze. Indeed, Chumpton Town appeared to be very nearly asleep; but this was perhaps partially due to the fact that Mr Ruby arrived on early-closing day. On early-closing day at Chumpton you have even to call for your own letters at the post office, as the postman is umpiring at cricket, and would be playing if he were not lame.

But Mr Ruby approved this lethargy. In his eyes Chumpton seemed to possess a blissful air of lotus-eating repose dear to his nature. He had now tramped the roads of the United Kingdom continuously for over thirty years, and by this time he possessed a pretty shrewd eye for hospitality. Chumpton struck him as about the softest thing in all the gentle west country. He progressed slowly but with confidence towards the market square, in boots acquired from the back-yards of two separate, outsize, unconscious benefactors.

Chumpton, however, has small use for the loafer. Standing on the make-believe sea-coast of Bridgwater Bay, it is far enough from the madding crowd to disdain the latter's ignoble strife, but its inhabitants are serene rather than idle. On the contrary, every man in the place wurrks. He may not wurrk quite so quickly as some of the madding crowd's misguided and early-dying wurrkers wurrk, but so much the better. Slow and sure is Chumpton's motto. The slower you wurrk, the surer is the wurrk to keep on waiting to be done.

Even in the residential quarter of Swallow Road there is always something doing. The retired sons of Mars fight many a grim battle over again on the golf course; while their Amazonian wives conduct slightly more refined but no less embittered feuds across the bridge table. Before now, some dashing young blood in a noisy runabout and a Fair Isle has swooped into Chumpton, slashed gashes in it with a mid-iron, and sailed off again, describing the place as sleepy. Sleepy! You wait till you meet Admiral Juddy and Colonel Rust, all square at the turn and rounding the bend for home in the teeth of a nor'-westerly hailstorm, and ask either of their caddies whether Chumpton is sleepy. You hang about in the ladies' club-house when Miss Edyth Creepe is playing a hand, with Mrs Mantle Ham's cards on the table, and wait until the last trick is turned and Dummy is allowed to speak. Nay, Chumpton sleeps not.

Mr Ruby made exactly the same mistake as the Fair Isle boy; he underrated Chumpton. The combination of dirt and stubble which decorated all the lower portion of his face parted in a sociable grin for such natives as he encountered; until, on gaining the precincts of the 'Bull and Battleaxe,' he hovered listlessly – rather in the manner of some devotee of etiquette seeking a desirable introduction.

Here, for the first time, he received the due recognition of the Chumpton authorities. The constable on duty showed him the almost incredible spectacle of a boot larger than either of his own. From the latter pair accordingly was shed the dust of Chumpton Town without question or delay. Ruby proceeded more rapidly than was his wont up Swallow Road to the sand dunes, and sought again the kindly and familiar company of Nature. He still grinned. Tell me this: Was it his tramping that made a philosopher of Autolycus, or was it his philosophy that turned him into a tramp?

Abnormally brisk exercise had made Ruby weary, and, choosing a commodious hillock in the thick, reedy grass, he stretched his limbs for a siesta. By mounting his hillock he could have obtained a glorious view, across the bay, of the Mendips tinted by the fickle sunlight of a showery May afternoon. But Ruby had grown somewhat blasé concerning the face of Nature; even as a husband, long wedded, comes to regard the beauty of his wife as an almost tedious matter-of-course.

He dozed placidly to awaken with a start. He was no longer alone. Strange sounds of some sort of fatigued hunting issued from the other side of the hillock. Snatches of some outlandish foreign blasphemy punctuated the hunting noises. A mysterious business. One thing alone was clear: someone was in trouble.

Other people's trouble had been the source of many an unconsidered trifle to Ruby. It was nothing short of a duty to investigate and sympathise. A nuisance, when he was just enjoying a pleasant nap; but it was about the first job he'd been called upon to do that day, so he couldn't complain. He peered over the top of the hillock, and gradually the light of truth dawned upon his intelligence.

This was it. The place where he'd been taking his doze was in the neighbourhood of one of them open stretches of country over which favoured blokes amazingly walk, pursuing a small white ball and walloping it. In the present case a bloke had walloped wide, with the result that he was now very heatedly exploring the rich, long grass in the vicinity of Ruby's hillock and probing it remorselessly with his hockey bat. The kid who bore the bag of spare bats was also searching, but considerably in the rear of the walloper.

The latter's countenance was not for the moment fully

revealed to Ruby; but a beard, bent shoulders and a certain angularity of leg argued age in addition to his other misfortunes. Sympathy was unquestionably indicated. ''Ave yer lorst yer little ball?' asked Ruby.

Admiral Juddy looked up. From a face purple with rage and effort shot a glance like a living flame of fire. The voice that had struck terror into the heart of every sub-lieutenant in the China Fleet made reply to Ruby. It spake as follows:

'What the crimson, p'twee, pong-choo blazes do you suppose I've done? May dogs defile your dhobi! M'sai muncha – go away – go on – diam – get away, blast you – you dirty-looking son of a coolie! Go on! P'twee! Poo!'

Now, Britannia rules the waves and all that; and hearts of oak are our men, and Jack's the Boy and so on – I quite admit that; but I have a sneaking idea, which I expect a great many other people are secretly nursing too, that the glamour surrounding the British Naval Officer has been a trifle overdone. Particularly does this apply to the B.N.O.'s of riper years. By the time one of them reaches the age of Admiral Juddy the pomposities of discipline have entered so deeply into his soul (while his constitution has been steadily undermined by gin) that he becomes liable to over-estimate his importance, his capabilities, and his licence to make remarks to anyone about anything in any language. It's all very well, but some of these old N.O.'s ought to try and remember that Britannia's object in ruling the waves is to prevent Britons from ever, ever, ever becoming slaves. To them or anybody else.

Ruby was piqued. The village copper had booted him out of the market square. That was all right; that was the legitimate and well-recognised function of the copper. But that here, in the open country, under God's clear sky, a fellow-creature should deliberately shout at him and tell him to m'sai muncha – this was intolerable. He was bitterly annoyed at it.

He retaliated by seating himself on the top of the hillock and silently baiting Admiral Juddy, who returned to his search scowling from beneath his bushy eyebrows, audibly muttering some very vulgar Cantonese, and prodding his own foot rather severely by mistake with his niblick.

The seventeenth hole at Chumpton is in many respects

typical of Life in general. You can see only a very little way ahead of you. A tall hill confronts you as you stand on the tee, and you have to get over the middle of that hill. The way is not long, but ah! it is strait and narrow. If you slice, there are bunkers deep; if you pull, there is tiger country. It is almost exactly like a thing out of the 'Pilgrim's Progress'.

Admiral Juddy's opponent was a Mr Twine, a good Christian but, like so many of the better Christians an indifferent golfer. A fair, average, heathen eight-handicap man could reach the green from the tee with a mashie iron. Mr Twine, by means of a full blow with a Dreadnought driver, had managed to hit his ball as far as the right-hand bunkers, whither he had now proceeded. Admiral Juddy's caddie, who in the course of the afternoon had heard a lot of new and startling information concerning himself, was looking for the lost ball with but little enthusiasm and an implied cynicism regarding the length of the Admiral's tee-shot. The Admiral himself delved and cursed in the tiger country. Ruby grinned from his hillock. And at this point Miss Kyte, most strapping and masculine of all the up-to-date strapping and masculine daughters of St Andrew, teed her ball on the seventeenth tee, tossed her cigarette to the ground, addressed, swung and smote.

She carried her own clubs, preferring to dispense with a caddie. So did her opponent, Young Harry Chinney, an assistant preparatory schoolmaster, who couldn't afford one. But there was no need to explore. The Admiral and Mr Twine must either have played the hole by this time or have lost a ball. Miss Kyte accordingly smote.

Her ball curled over the tall hill and away to the left. With it we take flight from the strait and narrow line of reason into an adventure of the wildest improbability.

Admiral Juddy waded out of the worst of the tiger country and stood on a bank of smooth, short grass, breathing great snorts of rage from his nostrils like a very old and very angry dog. His caddie had now, perhaps in self-defence, entirely disappeared. Twine was one down and would take at least six to get out of the bunker, and would have lost the match for a certainty. Now he would have to be presented with the hole. It wasn't that the Admiral minded losing a ball or a hole or a match, or anything else. It was simply blast and curse life in general, and golf in particular. Why the multi-coloured eternity of woe was one such a fool as to play golf, or, if it came to that, to live this blasted life? Oh, completely, finally and eternally, blast and damn everything!

Miss Kyte's ball fell with a thud behind him and came bouncing gaily along the grass. A great spasm of rage shook every nerve in Admiral Juddy's frame. That one should live and golf was bad enough. That one should be smitten into without warning in this off-hand manner, and at this moment accursed, was literally pswee-ho. Blind with fury, the Admiral slashed wildly at Miss Kyte's perky little bouncer with his murderous niblick. He hit it.

It sailed, spinning merrily, into the air again. It fell on the green, bounced, ran, settled into a staid trickle, trickled to the edge of the hole, hesitated coquettishly and flopped home.

Next moment Twine, a short, agreeable gentleman, who should never have worn plus fours with those legs, and should have forsworn a drooping moustache, but who was very well-meaning and affable, came trotting eagerly towards the tiger country.

'Oh, good shot indeed!' he cried. 'Beautiful! My word! In the hole – absolutely in! I was just coming over to help you find the ball. I suppose that's only your second? I'm on the green, but I've played five. Well done, I say. A magnificent shot!'

To each of us comes the devil at his chosen moment. Oh, don't dispute it – you sin; I sin; we all of us know that insidious whisper, and yield to it; and who are we to judge others? At that moment, quelling the fire and tempest of wrath and sorrow, whispered the subtle voice of the tempter into the rather reddened ears of Admiral Juddy.

He pulled his beard, frowned at the gushing Twine. For a fatal second he wavered. The fatal second gave birth to another, during which he shot a quick glance towards the spot where he had last seen his caddie. The caddie had reappeared, but his back was turned, and he was still searching listlessly. Admiral Juddy toyed with Satan.

'It certainly was a pretty good shot,' he muttered.

'Marvellous!' agreed Twine. 'Well, well, that's the match; but I don't mind losing to a shot like that. Hallo, here's somebody playing behind us!'

As he spoke, Mr Chinney gained the top of the high hill guarding the green, where he proceeded calmly to play several shots without further notice; while round the foot of the hill came the striding and swinging figure of Miss Kyte.

'I suppose they think we've lost a ball,' said Twine, with a nervous smile at Admiral Juddy. The latter, overcome perhaps by his supreme effort with the niblick, exhibited an unusual hesitation to move on.

'It – er – it *was* your shot, wasn't it?' asked Twine.

'Hell d'yer mean?'

'What? I mean – it *was* you that hit that ball, that ball that went into the hole, that *was* you?'

'Of *course* I flaming well hit it! What the ——?'

'Exactly. Quite. Well done. Only, I mean – shan't we go on?'

Admiral Juddy decided mentally upon a compromise. At a more convenient moment he would reveal the truth to Twine. But as for this swaggering hoyden with her confounded presumption, bursting in upon him with a cigarette in her mouth and practically knickerbockers on her legs, he would teach her a lesson. She could dashed well stay and find his ball, and he'd carry on with hers. Serve her right, the dragon's whelp! With an oath of summons to his caddie, he turned towards the green.

'Seen my pill?' inquired Miss Kyte.

'No,' replied Twine pleasantly.

'Found your own, then?'

'Ye-es,' said Twine. 'Admiral Juddy has just found his and played it. Magnificent shot too. Holed it from here.'

'Oh, come on!' commanded Admiral Juddy. 'Don't stand gossiping there. And another time,' he added, addressing Miss Kyte, 'you kindly wait till I'm off the green.'

'Well, look nippier,' said Miss Kyte. 'Besides, if you were standing here, I must have almost hit you. Are you sure you didn't play my ball by mistake?'

'I can positively swear to that,' replied the Admiral. 'Twine, will you come on? Caddie, come on, will you? Come on; run, you son of a duck!'

'What ball were you playing with – a Dunlop?' asked Miss Kyte.

'Yes. Why?'

'Yes? So was I. What number?'

'What number was yours?'

'Four, said Miss Kyte.

'So was mine,' said Admiral Juddy. 'So pung-ti to *that*.'

He stumped away. 'Hell!' said Miss Kyte and, throwing her golf-bag aside, plunged into the tiger country.

Ruby shifted his position on the hillock. He watched the Admiral out of earshot; then from between his teeth uttered a low whistle. Miss Kyte raised her head.

'Hi!' said Ruby in a tone of hoarse confidence. 'Here! Hi! Mister!'

When the Admiral won the eighteenth, holing a skilful two-foot putt for a nine, while Twine could only accomplish a hovering ten, again, and with greater subtlety than before, whispered the evil one. The match would have been won in any case. Suppose Twine learnt the truth, only to be cross-questioned subsequently by that cocky and pugnacious young woman – Twine would have wantonly to lie to Miss Kyte. Was this fair to Twine – a man of a high moral standard? No, no; the Admiral shrunk from placing his friend in so distasteful a situation. Besides, the fool might blurt out the secret.

So Admiral Juddy quaffed the fruits of victory at the bar, cut short with unwonted modesty Twine's amiable efforts to recount in public the details of that wonderful approach, and stalked into the card-room to scent out likely victims in another field.

Ten minutes later he was beginning to feel quite pleased with life again. He cut with Major Heathcote-Bigge against Twine and Ramsbotham, which was, for a start, satisfactory to the Admiral and, secretly, very satisfactory to Twine. Without asking any support from the junior service, Admiral Juddy had already won four tricks in shovels, and had doubled and devastated a rash experiment in three sparklers on the part of

Ramsbotham. He had just dealt, and essayed a cautious opening to the tune of a couple of bludgeons, when young Chinney entered the card-room with an air of affront and stood beside the Admiral's chair. The nautical pulse beat a trifle more rapidly, but Admiral Juddy betrayed no interest in young Chinney.

'May I speak to you a moment outside, please, Admiral?' said the latter.

'Whaa?' said Admiral Juddy. 'Outside? Hell d'yer mean? No, certainly not. Nor inside either. Get out!'

'Well, I'm sorry; but it's rather a serious business. Miss Kyte says you deliberately played her ball at the seventeenth and wants to see you about it.'

Admiral Juddy laid his cards face downwards on the table. His face loomed upwards, extra veins appearing in several places.

''Sh!' said Twine in intelligent anticipation. ''Sh! No, no. Steady, I say.'

Admiral Juddy delivered himself of a message to Miss Kyte which would have startled a Mercantile Marine skipper.

'I'm sorry,' said Harry Chinney. 'It's nothing to do with me. But Miss Kyte says unless you give her an explanation she'll go to the Secretary.'

'If she wants to know where to go ——' said Admiral Juddy.

'Yes, yes,' said Twine. 'Now, now.'

Admiral Juddy gripped the sides of his chair and swung round savagely at Harry Chinney.

'Hell's grid!' he cried. 'Get out of this before I become annoyed!'

Next time an unwilling steward was detailed for the post of messenger. Tact prompted him to adopt stooping and whispering methods with the Admiral; but he rather unwisely waited until the latter had finished losing four doubled tricks in bloodthumpers. He then approached very diffidently and did his stooping and whispering.

'The Secretary's compliments, sir; and would you see him for a moment in his room?'

Admiral Juddy fisted the table.

'Pow-chee to the Secretary, and bong-ho to you!' he roared.

'Is this – ah – still to do with Miss Kyte?' inquired Major Heathcote-Bigge, a well-connected pauper residing aimlessly at Chumpton and applying himself very seriously to a variety of trivial affairs.

'Miss Kyte is in the Secretary's room, sir,' admitted the steward.

'Well, by Jove, Juddy, I think you should take action in this mattah,' said Major Heathcote-Bigge. 'I thought so before, only I didn't like to say so. It's simply unwarrantable that a girl like that should walk into the club and launch poisonous accusations against one of its very oldest membahs.'

'What do you mean – very oldest?' demanded Admiral Juddy.

'One of its membahs of the longest standing. It's too fearfully thick. The girl should be shot out.'

'If you'll excuse my saying so, sir,' said the steward, 'I happened to overhear Miss Kyte remark to the Secretary that she thought Admiral Juddy was afraid to come and see her.'

'Yes,' said Twine hastily. 'Whose deal is it?' But the Admiral's chair had already shot to the wall.

'What else did she say?' inquired the Major.

'She said, sir, that she could prove that Admiral Juddy played her ball, sir. I'm only saying what she said, sir.'

Admiral Juddy made no comment. He merely pushed the steward across the card-room, flung back the door and went forth to action.

Major Heathcote-Bigge also rose. 'I'm going to have a squint at this,' he remarked authoritatively. 'It may become a committee mattah.'

It practically became this forthwith; for members of the committee in all parts of the building heard the uproar which was taking place in the Secretary's room, and met there to deal with it. On Admiral Juddy first pausing to take breath it was proposed by the assistant hon. treasurer that he should confine his remarks to the English language, but upon his proceeding to do so this motion was lost by a large majority. A vice-president then proposed that Admiral Juddy should allow Miss Kyte to state the nature of her complaint. This was agreed to. But only by the committee.

At length, however, Miss Kyte's story was told, and it was realised at once that here was a crisis that would shake the social and sporting world of Chumpton to the marrow. The evidence of Twine was sought, but proved to be rather futile. 'I mean, beyond it being the most marvellous shot I've ever seen, I really can't say anything, because, I mean, I didn't actually see it. I mean, naturally, I didn't, because, you see, I was over the other side of the course. I mean, you see, naturally, I was in the bunker.'

'Well,' said Miss Kyte, throwing a decisive cigarette-end into the Secretary's inkpot, 'listen here. I'll give him a chance. If he cares to admit he lost his wool and dotted my Dunlop as it ran by, I'll say done finish.' She paused. Several strong men held Admiral Juddy.

'If he doesn't,' continued Miss Kyte, 'either he or I have got to bung out of this club. The committee will please sit tomorrow and decide which it's to be. Is that a bet?'

'Come, come, Miss Kyte,' said another vice-president; 'it is simply a question of hard swearing between you ——'

'Yes,' said Admiral Juddy. 'I've just thought of one or two things she hasn't heard yet.'

'It isn't!' cried Miss Kyte. 'I can bring proof. Somebody saw him hit my ball as it ran by him.'

'Who?' inquired several voices at once.

'A membah?' demanded Major Heathcote-Bigge, a stalwart pro-Juddite.

'No; but a perfectly unprejudiced and reliable sort of blighter,' retorted Miss Kyte.

'Who is he? Where is he now? Why don't you trot him along now?' they challenged; but Miss Kyte stood firm.

'I couldn't bring him into the clubhouse, and I'm blowed if I'm going to slog all the way back to find him. No, I'll get him by tomorrow. Go on; you can't refuse me a fair inquiry. If you do, it simply means that you know that one of your pet nuisances has been pretty badly caught out and you've all got the breeze up.'

'No, no; I say; 'sh! Oh, tut, tut, *please*, tut, tut!' breathed Twine anxiously to the Admiral. 'After all, she *is* a lady.'

*　　*　　*

They compromised by appointing a sub-committee consisting of two very tactful vice-presidents, the Secretary and a deaf ex-vice-captain, with Major Heathcote-Bigge as chairman, to deal with the troublesome affair at 2.30 on the following afternoon. But by this time, it was hoped, the quarrel would have been settled out of court. It was not very clear who actually hoped this, but presumably it was the deaf ex-vice-captain. Miss Kyte withdrew proudly, repeating her promise to furnish a witness on the morrow. Admiral Juddy had two or three pick-me-ups and stumped home alone, more bent and beard-pulling than usual. 'Poor old Juddy,' remarked a member. 'He seems to have taken it quite to heart.'

Truth to tell, the Admiral was far from tranquil. The voice of conscience? Well, not exactly. In fact, very little did the voice of conscience worry him. P'twee to the voice of conscience. But if only he could possibly discover who the devil had seen him hit that ball!

Ruby, with one half-crown in his pocket, and the promise of another if he would turn up at a stated address at a given time, was already on his way to the house where dwelt this surprising, munificent he-woman. It was understood that he was to receive further orders, involving further half-crowns. A pleasant business, this – profitable without savouring at all distastefully of work. The red house at the third corner – this was it. He entered at the back gate, and was bitten by a dog; but Miss Kyte put her head out of the first floor and bade him welcome. She then went below, reprimanded the dog, surprised the cook, took Mr Ruby into the scullery and offered him beer. Ruby blinked. Was this still the same hard world?

He got his second half-crown, but the further orders had not been issued before Miss Kyte was hastily sent for by Mrs Kyte. The cook was giving notice. So the benefactress told Ruby to wait at the corner of the garden, where, after soothing cook, she would join him.

Very bent, brow-furrowed and bitterly muttering, along the Swallow Road came Admiral Juddy. At the corner where dwelt the accursed Kytes the name of the road became to his ears strangely justified, for from the hedge came the sound of rich, deep and grateful swallowing. He peered, scowling.

Then enlightenment, like a burst of sunlight, banished the clouds of perplexity from his expression.

The scum —— Of course that was it! The scum had watched him from that hillock and had informed against him. And the woman had had the unspeakable effrontery to believe the word of the scum rather than the word of a retired admiral of His Majesty's Navy. And here was the scum being petted and cajoled with malted bribery against the fatal morrow.

Conscience (even when p'tweed into silence) makes cowards of us all. Admiral Juddy gripped his stick tightly in order to master his true emotions and addressed Ruby. He said:

'Is that beer?'

Ruby replied with an affirmative wink.

'D'yer like beer?'

'Ah-h!' said Ruby from his very stomach.

'I saw you on the golf links this afternoon, I believe?' said Admiral Juddy. 'Spoke a bit curtly, I fancy? I was a trifle annoyed at the time. Don't want to appear hard on yer. Come down to my house and you shall drink as much beer as you can.'

Ruby fingered his stubble pensively. He mistrusted this bloke. He greatly preferred the he-woman. But as much beer as he could ——! Yes, his first instinct had been true. Chumpton was the place. Only you wanted to ignore the town end and dwell in luxury up here among the toffs.

'As much as you can,' repeated the Admiral seductively. 'How much beer can you drink?'

'How much 'ave yer got?' replied Ruby.

'No, you don't,' said Miss Kyte, appearing in the hedge beside him.

'I wasn't going 'ome wiv 'im, sir, miss; I wasn't, straight,' protested Ruby. 'I'd rarver stay 'ere wiv you, arter what 'e called me this arternoon. You're my tally. I knows a genneman when I sees one – a lady – a ge – a gennle lady.'

'Trying to suborn my witness; that's fixed you,' said Miss Kyte. 'You're for it tomorrow.'

Fury, in full force, returned to Admiral Juddy.

'You're going to dare to bring this – pung-wee – this son of a mud-sweeper into the club-house to testify against *me*?' he shouted.

'Yes. You've given yourself away, offering him beer like that.'

'So have you!' cried Admiral Juddy. 'So have you, by the temple of the holy snake! If you bring this blot before the committee tomorrow I shall say I saw you with him in your garden last night, priming him with lies and swilling him with beer. I'll bring proof ——' The Admiral's voice rose to a roar like that of the last portion of a bath running out. 'Twine!'

Miss Kyte craned over the hedge. A knickerbockered figure in the middle distance of Swallow Road hesitated, and then unwillingly approached.

She took quick, frowning stock of Ruby. During this interlude he was searching the sides of his upturned glass for dregs with a pessimistic tongue. It *would* be rather undignified. On the other hand, the Admiral had played her ball and lied and basely counter-accused. He saw her waver, and pressed home his advantage with a lively prediction of the sub-committee's comments concerning her witness. But she boldly returned to the attack.

'Come on, now,' she said, 'get if off your chest. You got your shirt out and saw red and biffed my ball and, by a fluke in a million, holed it, and then had the almighty nerve to try and get away with it. I believed this tramp's word before yours, and now I've caught you trying to bribe him and proved I was a good judge. If that isn't sufficient humiliation for you, it ought to be. All right; I'll resign from the blinking club.'

'No, steady on; we can't have that,' said Admiral Juddy. 'Look here; will you accept an apology – a strictly private apology, mind you – and forget the whole confounded thing?'

'I don't mind your getting wild and hitting my ball,' said Miss Kyte. 'But lying about it like that – just because you did the hole in two.'

'What!' cried the Admiral. 'That wasn't the reason at all. Good Lord, I've done that hole in two scores of times! It was simply that – well – it was rather a headstrong thing to have done, and I didn't feel like admitting it.'

'I see,' said Miss Kyte. 'All right; call it off.'

'Oo do I get the beer from now, then?' asked Ruby.

'Hallo?' said Twine. 'Did you call me? What's up?'

The Admiral swung on him. 'Go away, damn you!' he said.

Major Heathcote-Bigge expressed gratitude that the little difference of opinion had been honourably settled, and that Miss Kyte had decided not to place the committee in the social quandary of having to listen to evidence against a membah from a witness who, it was understood, was not a membah. But, as a matter of fact, Ruby was at that moment, if not a membah, at least affiliated. For he was spending the afternoon beneath his favoured hillock, whither he had, indeed, immediately returned after witnessing the peace treaty of Swallow Road. No further orders had been forthcoming, but he had extracted a final half-crown from Miss Kyte in lieu; while an inspired attempt to pursue and blackmail Admiral Juddy on his own account had surprisingly caught the British Navy in melting mood and had produced further largess.

Ruby remained all that day and night beneath the shade of the hillock. No further miracles came his way, nor, perhaps, would he have regarded them had they done so. For when he arose early the next morning no wealth remained to jingle in his ragged pocket; but in the rich, long grass at the foot of the hillock lay in copious disorder bottles, bottles. He yawned, stretched his limbs, and philosophically set out to continue his lifelong tour of the United Kingdom.

18

A HEAVENLY ROUND

by Paul Gallico

THIS amusing story of 'golf-after-death' makes an ideal 18th hole for our round, offering as it does the suggestion that there just might be a special golf course in the sky where a golfer could turn a life-long passion for the game into an eternity! For 12 years Gallico was one of America's leading sports editors on the New York *Daily News* and could number among his friends some of the greatest golfers of the last few decades. He became internationally successful when he turned to novel writing and published the very popular story, *The Snow Goose*, in 1941.

Paul Gallico played a good round of golf himself, and won a number of local club competitions in New York State. He actually wrote 'A Heavenly Round' some years before his death in 1976, and one would like to think that he is now enjoying the same happy games as his hero, Barnaby Jessup, in the wide blue yonder. Or at least recalling some favourite moments in the great celestial club-house in the sky!

A HEAVENLY ROUND

The funeral was mighty impressive. It was bound to be in the case of a man like Barnaby Jessup. Most of the town had turned out, and after it was all over, one of the pallbearers looked up at the sky and murmured, 'Be a nice afternoon for golf.'

That remark might be considered to bear on the sacrilegious, in view of the occasion, but none of the other pallbearers objected, and they were all old friends of Barnaby Jessup, men in their sixties or higher, all but one of them, and Barnaby Jessup had been seventy-six when they laid him to rest.

The six pallbearers walked back across the gravel path to the car to take them back to town, and on the sidelines their names were spoken in hushed tones. For one of them, some years before, had been a candidate for president of the United States, one was a great surgeon in the land, a third, the young man of the lot, was a lean and tanned golf professional, winner of the Open, and it was he who had made the remark about golf.

The men got into the car and, as was natural, they talked about Barnaby Jessup on the ride back to town. But they did not reminisce about the time back in the 20's that Jessup had made a million in the stock market, nor about the way he had juggled railroads; it was of quite different matters that they talked.

The man who had almost become president, said, 'I was with Barnaby the day he put eight straight balls in the lake hole.'

The surgeon, his eyes reflective, said thoughtfully, 'I played with him the day he took a twenty-seven on a par-three hundred-and-ten-yard hole.'

The mildest man of the group, the man who was simply the head of one of the late Jessup's holding companies, said, 'I saw him wrap all of his clubs around a tree one afternoon,' and no one commented, because that had been commonplace.

The car hummed across the black ribbon of road and there was a silence while the men privately considered their friend, and then finally the golf professional looked up at the warm blue sky and spoke quietly.

'I hope Barnaby finds a golf course,' he said.

The gate before which Barnaby found himself was highly ornamental, of a curiously intricate wrought iron, and the pillars were of marble, but a marble which Jessup had never seen, marble with the lustre of a pearl.

'Ought to look into this,' Jessup said. 'The trustees could use it for the art museum.'

And so saying, he passed through the gate and was presently standing in the registrar's office, where in due time he gave his name to the clerk, who wrote it down in gold letters.

'Glad to have you with us, Mr Jessup,' the clerk said. 'A good many of the inmates like to know why they've been able to come here. In your case ——'

Jessup stopped him with a wave of the hand.

Like many men who have achieved great wealth and prominence, he was inclined to be autocratic. 'I left an art museum behind,' he said. 'I divided my fortune among colleges and institutions ——'

'Not for any of those things did you enter here,' said the clerk.

Jessup was momentarily startled. 'Well,' he said, 'I built the finest hospital in my state, equipped it with the best that money could buy, and brought some of the greatest medical men in the world ——'

The clerk said, 'That is entered on page three thousand one hundred and forty-nine under the heading Superficial Trivia.'

Jessup was jarred right down to his heels by that one. He thought a minute and then began a recital of what he had done with his money, the charities he had supported, and before he had gotten under way with the list the clerk was shaking his head negatively.

'You remember Jim Dolan?' said the clerk.

Jessup thought back down the years. 'Jim Dolan,' Jessup said slowly. 'Must have been thirty years ago, that was. He was a caddie at the club. Killed in an accident.'

'You went to see his mother,' the clerk said, reading aloud from a page in the ledger. 'You had a meeting that was worth thousands to you, and you turned it down to go and see his mother.'

'I didn't give her a dime,' Jessup said. 'Just called to pay my respects and tell her what a fine boy Jim had been. That's all I did.'

'That's all,' said the clerk gently, and smiled, and Barnaby Jessup scratched his head and wondered, but not for long, because he was a man of action and unaccustomed to being introspective.

'Look, son,' he said, 'all my life I've been on the go. I don't mean any offence, but tell me this, do I have to sit around on a cloud? I mean, just sit? And I've no ear for music, I can't play a harmonica, let alone a harp.'

'Why, no,' the clerk said. 'You can do about anything you like; anything within reason, that is.'

Barnaby hesitated and said in a low voice, 'No golf courses in these parts, I suppose?'

'No country clubs,' the clerk said. 'There's no discrimination up here. But we have a very fine public course.'

Barnaby Jessup smiled and then said, 'I didn't bring my clubs. I ——'

'Last door down on your left,' the clerk said.

Barnaby had another question, but he kept it back because

he didn't like to take too much of the clerk's time. And likely Pete Tyson wouldn't be up here anyway. Barnaby and Tyson had been business competitors and had fought each other with no rules and no holds barred, but most of all they had battled on the golf course. Ten years before, Barnaby had fought back the tears while he watched the clods go down over the mortal remains of his dearest enemy and closest friend.

He'd sure like to see old Pete. But a man can't have everything, he thought, and he went on down the hall to the last room on the left. A man sat at a bench inside and Barnaby stopped and stared, for he had never seen so many golf clubs. They lined the walls, clubs of every description.

'Help yourself,' the man at the bench said without looking up.

Barnaby thanked him and selected a likely-looking driver from a case along one wall. It had the right feel with the weight in the head where he liked it. He tried the rest of the clubs and found them perfectly matched, and finally he put the set in a golf bag and half a dozen balls in the pocket.

'What do I owe you?' he said, taking out his wallet and extracting two one-hundred-dollar bills, for these were hand-designed bench-made clubs and he was ready to pay two hundred for all he had there, but not a penny more because he had always made it a practice not to let people take advantage of him because of his wealth.

'No charge,' the man said, 'They're your clubs. Look on the shaft.'

Barnaby glanced down and saw his name stencilled there. 'Well,' he said in wonder, 'but look here, I want to give you something, I don't doubt all employees up here are well treated, but just the same ——'

The man squinted down the shaft of a club. 'I'm no employee,' he said. 'I'm a permanent resident and a busy man.'

Barnaby Jessup thanked him, walked to the door, then said, 'Can you tell me how to reach the course?'

'Six miles due north.'

'Is there a cab for hire?'

Barnaby couldn't understand what he said, it sounded like 'Fly,' and he didn't repeat the question, for the man was plainly eccentric, although a genius at his craft. He went outside to look for a cruising taxi and then he felt something at his back when he slung the golf bag over his shoulders and discovered that the strap was tangled up with a protuberance growing out of his shoulders.

He wiggled his shoulder blades, and the next thing he knew he was three feet off the ground and treading air, with both wings flapping.

'Well, I'll be,' Jessup said, then sighted on the sun, got a bearing on what he considered to be due north, and took off, flying at a steady, even clip about ten feet above the ground.

It was a trifle awkward; he got out of balance somehow while trying to shift the golf bag and went into a tailspin and landed on his chin in a gully, but it didn't hurt, and presently he was airborne again, and then finally he saw a long stretch of green ahead of him and he flew over the entire eighteen holes, surveying the layout.

When he had finished he knew he had just seen the ultimate in golf courses. The fairways were gently undulating, lush with grass, the greens like huge emeralds. It was a sporty course, too, not too flat, and yet not too hilly.

Getting quite excited, he flew back to the first tee, eager to swing a club, for although he had been one of the world's most successful men, it is said that no man achieves everything he wants in life and Barnaby Jessup had been a success at everything he turned his hand to with the exception of golf. A not inconsiderable part of his fortune had been spent on the game, but he had remained a duffer. He had in his home a comprehensive library of golf from the earliest works down to the most modern tomes. He had studied under the greatest professionals in the world and had built in the cellar of his home a cage where he would practice on such days that inclement weather kept him off the course. But he had remained a divot digger and a three putter down the years.

He made a neat two-point landing on the tee and as if by magic a caddie bobbed up, a small freckled boy with a missing front tooth who relieved him of his bag and handed him his driver.

'Howdy, Mr Jessup,' the boy said. 'Nice day for it.'

Jessup stared at him. 'Jim Dolan,' he said. He couldn't see any mark on the boy from the truck. 'Well, Jim,' he said, 'Like old days.'

'Smack 'er out there, Mr Jessup,' the boy said.

Jessup stood at the tee, addressing the ball and sighting toward the green, four hundred yards distant. Then he ran through the rules, cautioning himself not to press, to keep his head down, to start the club back low to the ground, to let the left arm do the work, to cock his wrists, and to shift his weight to the right foot with most of the weight on the heel.

He thought of all these things and then struck the ball, wincing a little as he always did, expecting either a hook or a slice. But he heard a musical little click, and the ball bounced on the fairway about two hundred and sixty yards away.

'Good shot,' Jim said.

'Best one I ever hit,' Jessup cried. 'By juniper, I had it that time. I think I've figured this game out.'

They walked forward to the ball and Jessup selected a brassie, sure that he was going to miss because never in his life had he put together two consecutive good shots.

He swung the brassie and that click sounded again and Jessup rubbed his eyes and said in awed tones, 'It's on the green.'

The caddie was already walking forward, handing Jessup his putter.

'I never made a par in my life,' Jessup said. 'I have a chance for a birdie. Oh, well, I suppose I'll three-putt.'

On the green he surveyed the situation, noticing the slope toward the pin. He jabbed at the ball, tightened up, but it rolled forward and fell into the cup.

Barnaby Jessup mopped his brow with a handkerchief and sat down on the apron at the edge of the green.

'Well,' he said finally, 'accidents will happen. Let's go, Jim. But maybe, at that, I will break one hundred today.'

The second was a water hole. The lake sparkled a bright sapphire in the sun and the distance across the water was a hundred and eighty yards.

Jessup selected a spoon. 'I should have brought more than six balls,' he said. 'Don't know why I didn't. I lose at least six every time I play. I'll put at least three in that lake.'

He swung, then listened for the whoosh as the water received his offering, but he failed to hear it and neither did he see drops of water splashing upward.

'Lost sight of it,' Jessup said.

'Good shot,' the caddie said. 'It's in the cup. It's a hole in one, Mr Jessup.'

'Now wait a minute, Jim,' Jessup said. 'You're not supposed to lie up here. Besides, I'm an old man ——'

'It's in the cup,' the boy repeated.

Jessup was looking for a path around the lake when the boy took off and flew across, and Jessup sailed after him. They landed on the green and sure enough the ball was in the cup.

He was too shocked to say anything, but assumed that every once in a while this kind of thing happened to everyone, a superlatively good day, but of course he'd go blooie any minute; he always had, he always would.

The next hole was three hundred and eighty yards and his drive was straight and far. They came up to it and the caddie handed him a seven iron.

'I usually use a five this far away,' Jessup said.

'You can make it with the seven,' Jim said.

Jessup didn't think so, but although he invariably took the hide off people who tried to advise him at business, he'd never somehow been able to disregard a caddie's advice.

Meekly he took the seven and swung. The ball landed on the edge of the green, bounced twice, rolled forward and fell into the cup. Jessup removed his glasses, blew on them and put them back on.

'You're playing a nice steady game,' the caddie said. 'Even two's at this point.'

'I am not,' Jessup said. 'Don't be ridiculous, Jim. I can't possibly have played three holes and only taken six shots. Nobody could, no golfer in the world.'

He took the scorecard from the boy and counted it, and counted it again on his fingers, and the boy was right, there was no disputing it. He had a three and a one and a two. There was no getting away from it. It wasn't possible, but there it was. He was even two's.

He had started out with the eternal hope of breaking one hundred. Now he was afraid to think about it. But still, he told himself, he'd go blooie any moment now.

And when they stood on the fourth tee he was sure of it. Despite the fact that he was in heaven, this hole might have been designed by the devil himself.

The fairway was perhaps forty yards wide with a dog leg in the distance. On the left was a gorge, the fairway ended abruptly, and beyond it was a vast nothingness; he could see clouds below it. A hooked ball was a goner.

'What happens to the ball if you hook it over the gorge?' Jessup said.

The boy's face was serious. 'It goes all the way down,' he said. 'All the way.'

'To the earth?' Jessup said.

And Jim Dolan shook his head. 'All the way down.'

Jessup took a second look and the clouds parted and he got a faint whiff of brimstone and saw a red glow burn madly for a moment.

'The only golf balls they get are the ones hooked over that gorge,' the caddie said. 'Poor devils.'

Jessup placed his ball on the tee. On the right were the densest woods he had ever seen, and the fairway itself was sprinkled with traps. He took careful aim at a grassy spot between two traps and swung. He was afraid to look, and automatically he was reaching in his hip pocket for a second ball when the caddie said, 'Nice shot.'

And there was the ball, dead in the middle of the fairway.

They walked towards it and Jessup was shaking as though he had the ague, although it was as nice a day as a golfer could find, no breeze and not too hot, just warm enough to make a man's muscles feel loose.

They had almost reached the ball when they heard a sound in the woods to the right and a moment later a handful of dirt and pebbles came down out of the sky and then a ball dropped out of nowhere and landed in front of them.

Barnaby stopped and looked around at a lean lanky figure

coming out of the woods. He had a turned-down mouth and a bald and wrinkled pate and he was talking to himself. 'By Saturn,' he said, 'by Venus, that was a shot.'

Barnaby stared in amazement and then finally he found his tongue. 'Pete Tyson, you old horsethief,' he said.

'Well,' Tyson cackled, 'I never expected to see you here. What did you do, bribe the authorities?'

They shook hands and grinned at each other and then Tyson addressed his ball and he hadn't changed at all, Barnaby saw. Tyson wound himself into a pretzel until he was next door to strangling himself, then the club came down and the ball hopped across the fairway and disappeared over the edge of the gorge and down towards the licking red flames.

But his old partner had become philosophical, Barnaby had to admit that, 'If it weren't for me,' Tyson muttered, 'they'd have a hell of a time down there.' And he took another ball from his hip pocket, placed it on the turf and hit it towards the pin.

It was like old times playing with Pete Tyson, and Barnaby was so puffed up he could hardly wait to hit his ball. He could hardly contain himself, waiting to see the look on Tyson's face when he showed him how he was hitting the ball now.

Jim Dolan handed him a brassie and Barnaby stepped up and swung, and when he raised his head the ball was lying on the green. He turned and looked at his friend and waited for him to say something.

But Tyson hadn't even opened his mouth. He just grunted and moved on down the fairway, and Barnaby stared at him, his face getting red.

They went along to the green and Barnaby sank a forty-foot putt and he looked up, and still Tyson didn't say a word, and that was the last straw.

They went towards the next tee and Barnaby exploded. 'Why don't you be a man?' he said. 'I always knew I was the better golfer and now I've proved it. Why can't you be man enough to admit it? Just standing there and sulking like the cantankerous old goat you are.'

'Hit the ball,' Tyson growled. 'If there's anything I hate it's a gabby golfer. You always did talk too much.'

His face purple now, Barnaby stepped up without another word and hit the longest drive ever seen in the solar system. The ball went practically out of sight, then came down on the green and Jim Dolan handed him his putter.

And still Tyson's expression hadn't changed. Barnaby stood there, choking, while Pete hit his usual hundred-yard drive into the rough. They plodded along and Barnaby couldn't figure how Tyson had gotten up here, but it was obviously a mistake, and somebody had slipped up somewhere; some mix-up in the celestial filing system probably explained it. And instead of being grateful Tyson was more ornery here than he'd ever been down below, which was saying a good deal. And maybe Tyson wouldn't admit it, but anyway, Barnaby was going to beat the tar out of him.

And he did. They finished the first nine and Barnaby totted up his score.

Pete Tyson said, 'Gives me a sixty-three. Couple of bad holes, but I'll do better on the back nine. Let's have an ambrosia before we start out.'

They walked up to the terrace and a waiter flew out with two tall and misty-looking glasses.

Barnaby put his score card down on the table. 'I have a twenty-three,' he said defiantly. 'The caddie will vouch for it. I'll shoot about a forty-five for the eighteen.'

He shoved the card under Tyson's nose, but the old goat just yawned and said nothing.

Barnaby sat there and told himself that he was the champion golfer of the universe. But somehow it left him cold, and suddenly he felt old and tired and even the ambrosia tasted flat. He sighed, put down his half-empty glass and got up slowly from the table.

'In a hurry?' Tyson grunted.

Barnaby said sadly, 'Sorry, Pete, but somehow I don't feel so good. I'm going to turn in my clubs. Don't think I'll play any more golf.' And he thought that even if Tyson had congratulated him, he still wouldn't want to play any more.

Pete's wise old eyes squinted up at him and he chuckled dryly.

'Barnaby, you old fool,' he said, 'I shot a forty-six myself the

[211]

first round I played here. It's one of the house rules.'

'House rules?' Barnaby said, bewildered.

'They let you have up here what you don't get below,' Tyson said. 'You always wanted to be a perfect golfer. So did I. But somehow, most of the residents prefer to go back to being themselves. You can make your choice.'

Barnaby didn't have to think twice for the answer to that one. And suddenly the sun came out and his loneliness was gone and he was itching to get out on the tee again.

'Tell you what,' Tyson said. 'On this back nine I'll play you for the ambrosia at the nineteenth. I'll give you three strokes.'

'You'll give me strokes!' Barnaby's face was purple again.

'You've gotten hogfat since I saw you,' Tyson said. 'And besides, I've had lessons from Macpherson.'

'Sandy Macpherson is up here?' Barnaby said in a whisper, for his was a name to conjure with.

'And where else would he be?' said Tyson. 'So it's only fair I give you strokes. I wouldn't take advantage of you.'

Barnaby's jowls shook with his laughter. 'You'll give me strokes! Do I look like a man that takes candy from a baby! I never saw the day when I had to take strokes from a string bean of a man put together with baling wire. Strokes! Come on,' he said. 'I'm playing you even!'

'Man, you'll rue the day,' said Tyson, and their scowls wavered for a minute and became broad grins as the love they had for each other came through.

The caddies came up and they hurried across to the tenth tee. 'Start it off,' Barnaby said. 'Give me something to shoot at if you can.'

Tyson wound up and he missed the ball on his first try and swung again and got himself bunkered behind the ladies' tee.

'If I couldn't do better than that,' Barnaby chuckled, 'I'd quit.'

He took his stance and then saw a stranger watching him, a hawk of a man with a blade for a nose, a man with sandy red hair, and shrewd grey eyes, and a pipe in his mouth and a contemptuous dour look on his face.

'Meet Sandy Macpherson, our pro,' Tyson said.

'Too bad we didn't meet earlier,' Barnaby said. 'I'd have

liked a lesson from you, but I'll not be needing one now, for I've finally grooved my swing.'

'Then swing, laddie, and dinna talk sae much,' said Macpherson.

Barnaby waggled his club over the ball and ran over the rules in his mind and started back with the left hand and kept his eye on the ball and pivoted with the hips and shoulders and did everything according to the book – or so he thought. But there was a whooshing sound like a wet sock falling on a concrete floor and the ball blooped into the air and came down in a meadow to the right of the fairway.

'You'll have to hit another,' Tyson cackled. 'The Elysian fields are out of bounds.'

Hit another he did, a topped dribbling shot and he turned to Sandy Macpherson.

'I'd better have a lesson tomorrow,' Barnaby said. 'I must have done something wrong.'

'Something!' said Macpherson with a laugh like a rusty safe door opening. 'Ye dinna keep yere head doon.'

'No, sir,' said Barnaby, humble and ashamed.

'Ye swing like an old witch wi' a broomstick.'

'I suppose I do,' Barnaby said meekly, bowing his head for shame.

'Hoot,' said Macpherson, 'I'll hae to throw yere game away, mon. I'll hae to start from scratch and see if there's aught to be done wi' ye. Ten o'clock sharp tomorrow.'

'Yes, sir,' said Barnaby, 'I'll be there.' He grinned at Tyson, who was grinning back at him, and then started out to hunt for his ball in the Elysian fields, whistling a tune of his youth, and happy as a lark.

IN THE CLUB-HOUSE

THIS FINAL SECTION of the book brings together three very different men, but all united by a common passion for the game of golf. Their observations on the sport are, I venture to suggest, similar to the sort of conversations that one might find in any club-house when the talk turns to the funny side of the game . . .

19

GOLF FOR DUFFERS

by Sir Henry Rider Haggard

RIDER HAGGARD, the famous author of such classic high adventure novels as *King Solomon's Mines* (1885), and the other stories of the great white hunter, Allan Quatermain, was the first English enthusiast of golf to write about the funny side of the game in this following essay, 'Golf For Duffers', which he contributed to the weekly magazine, *The Graphic*, of November 29, 1890. Haggard, who lived in Norfolk, had played on a number of courses in both England and Scotland, as well as meeting several of the most distinguished golfers of his time including the great Scotsman, Tom Morris, and the British statesman, A. J. Balfour, who was Prime Minister from 1902–6, and himself contributed a chapter on 'The Humours of Golf' to Harold Hutchinson's book, *Golf*, published in 1898.

'Golf for Duffers' is an entertaining, amusing and at the same time revealing piece about the state of the game in the Victorian era, and this marks its first re-publication in over a century.

GOLF FOR DUFFERS

Oh! well with thee, my brother,
  Who hast not known the game,
When early gleams of gladness
Aye set in after sadness;
And still the end is other,
  Far other, than the aim.
Oh! well with thee my brother
  Who hast not known the game

So, if memory does not deceive, runs the inspired lay of the
bard of the *Saturday Review*. It is of Golf that he sings, not of
Nap or Poker, or Pitch-farthing, or any other exciting, but
deceitful and deleterious sport. Many have sung and written
of it of late, and soon the searcher of bibliographies will find
the titles of a multitude of works under the heading 'Golf.'

'What,' said a friend to this writer the other day, as he took up Mr Horace Hutchinson's contribution to the Badminton Library, 'what, all that great book about hitting a little ball with a stick!' But this and other learned works are written by 'golfers of degree,' past masters in the art of 'hitting the little ball.' It yet remains for the subject to be treated from the other side, from the point of view, and, for the comfort of the Duffer. This, the present writer considers himself qualified to do, and for the best of reasons, he wots of none who can play worse than he.

Now as all men know, or ought to know, the game of golf consists in striking a small ball of some hard material into a series of holes – generally eighteen in number – with a variety of wooden and iron-headed clubs, which experience has proved to be the best adapted to the purpose. At first sight this looks easy enough. Indeed, strange as it may seem, the beginner sometimes does find it fairly easy – for the first time or two. He takes the driver with that beautiful confidence which is born of ignorance; hits at the ball somehow, and it goes – somehow; not a full drive of 180 yards or so, indeed, but still a very respectable distance. Arrived safely in the neighbourhood of the first green, he is told that he must putt the ball into a hole about the size of a jam pot. Perhaps he does it at the first attempt, and from a distance whence an experienced player would be quite content to lay his ball near the hole. Then he remarks that 'it seems pretty easy.' Probably his adversary will assent with a sardonic smile, and wait for the revenge that time will surely bring. He need not wait long; it may be today or tomorrow; but an hour will come when he will see the triumphant tyro scarcely able to hit the ball, much less to send it flying through the air, or wriggling sinuously into the putting-hole, perhaps from a dozen yards away. He will see him cutting up huge lumps of turf behind it – this diversion is called 'agriculture' – or smiting it on the head with such force as to drive it into the ground, or 'topping' it so that it rolls meekly into the nearest bush, or 'pulling' it into the dyke on the left, or 'toeing' it into the sand-bunker on the right; doing everything, in short, that he should not do, and leaving undone all those things that he should do. For days and weeks he will see him thus employed, and then, if he is a revengeful person, he will take some particularly suitable occasion, when the ball has been totally missed three or four times on the tee, say, to ask, if he, the tyro, 'really thinks golf so very easy.'

Let none be deceived – as golf is the most delightful game in the world, so it is also the most difficult. It is easier even for a person who has never handled a gun to learn to become a really good shot than for him who has not lifted cleek or driver to bloom into a golfer of the first water. To the young, indeed, all things are possible, but to few of those who begin after thirty will it ever be given to excel. By dint of hard practice and care, in the course of years they may become second or third-rate players, but for the most part their names will never appear as competitors in the great matches of the world of golf. To begin with, but a small proportion will ever acquire the correct 'swing,' that is the motion of the arms and club necessary to drive the ball far and sure. We have all heard of and seen the 'St Andrew's Swing,' but how many can practise it with the results common at St Andrew's and elsewhere among first-class players. When success attends in the swing, then the ball is topped or heeled, and when the ball goes off well, then the less said about the swing the better. It is instructive to watch any gathering of golfers made up for the most part of players who have not been bred to the game. The majority of them are content with the half-swing, they do not lift the club over the shoulder. If asked their reasons, they will say with truth, that there is only some thirty yards difference between a drive from a half and a drive from a full swing, and that the former is far easier and more certain than the latter. Quite so, but it is not the game; and he who aspires to learn to play the game will prefer to swing full and fail gloriously rather than to attain a moderate success in this fashion. But the swing is only one of a hundred arts that have to be learned before a man can pretend to play golf. Till he has mastered these, or a goodly proportion of them, he does not play, he only knocks a ball along, a humble amusement with which alas! most of us must needs be content for the term of our natural lives. Golf, like Art, is a goddess whom we must woo from early youth if we would win her; we must even be born to her worship. No other skill will avail us here, the most brilliant cricketer does not necessarily make a first-class golfer; on the contrary, he must begin by forgetting his cricket; he must not lift himself on his toes and *hit* like a batsman making a drive. Doubtless, the eye which helps a man to excel in shooting, at tennis, or cricket, will advantage him here to some extent, but, on the other hand, he will have much to forget, much to unlearn. He must clear his mind of all superstitions, he must humble his pride in the sand, and begin with a new heart and a meek spirit, well knowing that failure is his goal. For he will never, never learn to play – it is folly to expect otherwise. Each evening he will see his mistakes and avow amendment to himself and to his partner, and yet, when the morrow is done, will come home murmuring: –

> It was *last night* I swore to thee
> That fond impossibility.

Impossibility! For the middle-aged duffer this word sums it all.

It may be said, Then why have anything to do with such a hopeless sport? Let him who asks play golf once, and he will understand why. He will go on playing because he must. Drink, opium, gambling – from the clutches of all these it is possible to escape, but from golf, never! Has anybody ever seen a man who gave up golf? Certainly dead donkeys are more common than these. Be once beguiled to the investment of five shillings in a driver, and abandon hope. Your fate is sure. The driver will be broken in a week, but what will you be? You are doomed for life, or till limbs and eyesight fail you – doomed to strive continually to conquer an unconquerable game. Undoubtedly golf is not so innocent as it seems, it has dangerous possibilities. Can we not easily conceive a man middle-aged, happy, prosperous, regular in his attendance at business, and well satisfied with an annual outing at the seaside? And can we not picture him again after golf has laid its hold upon him? He is no longer happy for he plays not better and better, but worse and worse. Prosperity has gone, for the time that he should give to work he devotes to the pernicious sport. He has quarrelled with his wife, for has he not broken all the drawing-room china in the course of practising his 'swing' on Sundays, and estranged his friends, who can no longer endure to be bored with his eternal talk of golf? As for the annual outing, it does not satisfy him at all; cost what it will, he must be on the links five days out of every seven. There is no need to follow him further, or we might dwell on the scene, as yet far off, for this poison is slow, when battered, broken, bankrupt, his very clubs in pawn for a few shillings, he perambulates some third-rate links, no longer as a player, but in the capacity of a superannuated caddie. Here is matter of romance indeed: the motive is generously presented to any novelist weary of portraying the effects of drink and cards. 'The Golfer's End; or, The Demon Driver,' should prove an effective title.

And yet even for those who will never really master it, the game is worth the caddie. To begin with, it has this startling merit, the worse you play the more sport you get. If the fisherman slacks his line, and lets off the salmon, or the shooter misses the only woodcock clean, or the batsman is bowled first ball off a lob, there is an end of those particular delights. But when the golfer tops his ball, or trickles it into a furze-bush, or lands it in a sand-bunker, it is but the beginning of joy, for there it lies patiently awaiting a renewal of his maltreatment. His sport is only limited by the endurance of his muscle, or, perchance, of his clubs, and at the end of the round, whereas the accomplished player will have enjoyed but eighty or a hundred strokes, the duffer can proudly point to a total of twice that number. Moreover he has hurt no one, unless it be the caddie, or the feelings of his partner in a foursome. By the way, the wise duffer should make a point of playing alone, or search out an opponent of equal incapacity; he should not be led into foursomes with members of the golfing aristocracy, that is if he has a proper sense of pride, and a desire not to look ridiculous. He should even avoid the company of members of his own family on these occasions, lest it chance that they lose respect for a man and a father who repeatedly tries to hit a small ball with a stick with the most abject results, and is even betrayed by his failure into the use of

language foreign to the domestic hearth. Here is advice for
him who has been bitten of the mania. Let him select a
little-frequented inland links, and practice on them studiously
about two hundred days a year for three years or so, either
alone, or in the company of others of his own kidney. By this
time, unless he is even less gifted than the majority of begin-
ners, he will probably be able to play after a modest and
uncertain fashion. Then let him resort to some more fashionable green, and having invested in an entirely new set of clubs,
pose before the world as a novice to the game, for thus he will
escape the scorn of men. But let him not reverse the process.
Thus he who, in his ignorance or pride, takes train to Wimbledon, and in the presence of forty or fifty masters of the art,
solemnly misses the ball three times on the first tee, may
perchance never recover from the shock.

Nor will those years of effort and of failure be without their
own reward. He will have tramped his gorsey common till
every bush and sod is eloquent to him of some past adventure.
This is the short green, that by some marvellous accident he
once did in *one*, driving his ball from the tee even into the little
far-away putting-hole. Here is a spot which he can never pass
without a shudder, where he nearly killed his opponent's
caddie, that scornful boy who, for many days accustomed to
see him topping and putting his ball along from green to green,
remained unmoved by his warning shouts of 'fore,' till one
unlucky hour, when by some strange chance he drove full and
fair. Crack! went the ball from his brassy. Crack! it came full
on the youthful head thirty yards away, and then a yell of
agony, and a sickening vision of heels kicking wildly in the air,
and presently a sound of clinking silver coin. There, too, is the
exact place, whence for the first (and perhance the last) time
he drove over the beetling cliff, and out of the great bunker,
the long way too, not the ladies' way – a feat not often accomplished by the skilful. A hundred and ninety-one yards that
drive measured, though it is true an envious and long-legged
friend who had forced his own ball an inch deep into the sand
of the cliff, stepped it at a hundred and eighty-four. He can
never forget that supreme moment, it will be with him till his
dying hour. Our first large salmon safely brought to bank, a

boy's first rocketing pheasant, clean and coolly killed, these afford memories that draw as near to perfect happiness as anything in this imperfect world, but it may be doubted if they can compare to the sense of utter triumph, of ecstatic exhilaration with which, for the first time, we watch the ball, propelled by our unaided skill, soar swiftly over the horrid depths of an hitherto unconquered bunker. There is a tale – a true one, or it would not be produced here – that, being true, shall be told as an example of noble patience fitly crowned and celebrated.

A wanderer musing in a rugged place was, of a sudden, astonished to see and hear an old gentleman, bearing a curiously shaped stick, walking up and down and chanting the *Nunc Dimittis* as he walked. Moved by curiosity, he came to the aged singer, and asked,

'Why do you chant the *Nunc Dimittis* on the edge of this gulf?'

'For this reason, sir,' he answered, pointing to a golf-ball that lay upon the turf.' 'For seventeen years and more I have attempted almost daily, to drive a ball across that bunker, and but now I have succeeded for the first time. The object of my life is attained, and I am ready to die. That, sir, is why I sing.'

Then the wanderer took off his hat, and went away, marvelling at the infatuation of golfers.

It need scarcely be said that the foregoing remarks apply to, and are intended for, the consideration of male duffers. It would have been agreeable to extend them to the other sex, but space demands brevity. Golf is a man's game, but here, too, women assert their rights. Not that they are all fond of it; by no means. On the contrary, a young lady has been heard, and recently, to express her decided opinion that a law should be passed against its practice during the summer months. This was a lawn-tennis young lady. And another informed this writer that she held golf to be a 'horrid game, where everybody goes off like mad, glaring at a little ball, without a word for anybody.' Others, it is true, attack the question in a different spirit – they play, and play well. It is curious to observe their style; that they do everything wrong is obvious even to the male incompetent. They stand in front of the ball, they swing their club wildly in preparation, and finally bring it down with an action that suggests reminiscences of a cook jointing veal; but the ball goes, for these young ladies have a good eye and a strong arm. Perhaps no woman-player could ever attain to a really first-rate standard, for however vigorous she may be she cannot drive like a man. But with practice there seems to be no reason why she should not approach and putt as well as any man; and certainly she can talk golfing-shop with equal persistency.

And now this duffer will conclude with a word of advice to the world at large – that they should forthwith enter the noble fraternity of duffers, of those who try to play golf and cannot. They will never succeed – at least, not ten per cent of them will succeed. They will knock balls from green to green, and reverence Mr Horace Hutchinson more truly and deeply than the great ones of the earth are generally reverenced; that is all. But they will gain health and strength in the pursuit of a game which has all the advantages of sport without its expense and cruelty; they will note many a changing light on land and sea; and last, but not least, for several hours a week they will altogether forget their worries, together with Law, Art, Literature, or whatever wretched occupation the Fates have given it to them to follow in the pursuit of their daily bread. For soon – alas! too soon – the votary of golf – that great gift of Scotland to the world – will own but one ambition, an ambition but rarely to be attained. Thus, he will sing with the poet.

> Who list may grasp at greatness,
>   Who list may woo and wive;
> Wealth, wisdom, power, position –
> These make not my ambition.
> Nay but I pray for straightness,
>   And do desire to drive.
> Who list may grasp at greatness,
>   Who list may woo and wive.

20

LAUGHTER ON THE LINKS

by *Bernard Darwin*

Bᴇʀɴᴀʀᴅ Dᴀʀᴡɪɴ, the doyen of all golf writers, needs little introduction to most enthusiasts of the game. In fact, though, his contribution to sporting journalism as a whole has been much wider than the game itself, for it was his first report for *The Times* of May 23, 1907, headlined simply 'Golf and the Championship', that effectively introduced the concept of writing about sport rather than merely printing the basic facts and figures of events. This milestone in journalism was to prove the forerunner of what has become a veritable library of great writing on all the various types of sport from archery to yachting.

Darwin was actually a lawyer who abandoned the bar to write about the game which had absorbed his interest all of his life. He had begun playing golf when he was eight, he once confessed, and though as an adult he won several fairly major tournaments, he always thought his style was 'too flamboyant and juvenile'. Darwin generally wrote about golf with great seriousness, but he was well aware of the funny side, as he so skilfully demonstrates – somewhat at his own expense – in the following essay written for *The Times* of July 21, 1934.

LAUGHTER ON THE LINKS

A small scene came suddenly back to me the other day with startling clearness. My kind tutor at Cambridge and his wife used every October term to go through a most painful martyrdom. In the course of the term they asked to dinner all his new pupils at the rate of five freshmen at a time. Further, since freshmen, however miserable they may be can seldom pluck up courage to say 'Good-night' and go away, one third-year man was asked as well, both to perform this necessary function and generally to leaven the lump. On one occasion the proceedings became so lame and halting that our host and hostess introduced in despair the subject of a literary examination paper, in which one question related to famous bursts of laughter in literature. Amid a deathly silence I did my best by citing one from 'Pendennis,' and afterwards one of the party was heard describing the evening with the utmost horror, and his voice rose almost to a scream as he said. 'There was one fellow there who actually answered a bit of one question!'

This has nothing to do with golf, but I was reminded of it by golf. At that solemn game it is not considered right to burst into laughter over our enemy's misfortunes, and I have often been gratefully aware of the heroic efforts of my opponents not to laugh at me. At the last week-end, however, I was playing in a team match by foursomes, and if it could not perhaps be said of the players that they were 'grand gowfers a', nane better,' all of them could claim at least a reasonable degree of competence. Nevertheless there arose in the course of the two days three separate occasions on which it seemed almost permissible to guffaw loudly.

A GROTESQUE FINISH

The most remarkable of these instances was the halving of the last hole in seven strokes apiece. The story is so long that I can only tell parts of it. It was not a long hole, since it could be reached with a drive and a pitch, and it possessed a green of a type I do not like, having a back wall or two side walls. Parenthetically I do not like it because my own ball always seems to hover on the top of the wall and then drop over on the far side, whereas my opponent's, after a similar period of suspense, runs back and lies dead. A and B were dormy one on C and D, and both sides drove down the middle of the course. A played the odd, a shot which he described as 'quite good but not held up quite enough'; the ball fell over the right-hand side wall. C, determined to hold his shot up enough, hooked whole-heartedly. D, being convinced that A and B could not do worse than a 5, tried to be clever and get a 4; he was far too clever and failed to get over a bump.

The rest of the story of C and D's 7 is a little shadowy, and I will return to A and B. B said it would be safest to putt over the wall. He putted with such good will that the ball climbed the first wall at full speed, ran the whole width of the green, and vanished over the wall on the other side. A said he would also putt, but putt more temperately. He did, and the ball came back to his feet. B had the third putt, and again the ball almost scaled the summit but alas! failed to do so by the material inch. Then exclaimed A, in the manner of Lady Macbeth:

'Infirm of purpose! Give me the daggers.'

He played the fourth putt, and a great one it was, for the ball just, and only just, got over the wall, trickled down the far side, and lay dead. C and D, after nameless adventures, had a putt for a 6 and missed it. So A and B kept their lead of one, and both sides left the green apoplectic with laughter.

The other two incidents were by comparison prosaic. In one case an eminent personage, who has played in a Walker Cup match, missed the globe in a bunker; his object was presumably to hit the sand, but all he did hit was the air, for the club passed high over the ball. In the other a most excellent player was required to play a short pitch and run to an open green. What he did play was an 'explosion' shot through the green. His club stuck in the turf some inches behind the ball, which spouted gently into the air and fell down not more than 5ft. from the spot whence it had started.

OVER THE WALL

I can give no adequate explanation of these phenomena. I can only most solemnly assert that they occurred. Mr Snodgrass on a famous occasion explained that 'It was the salmon,' and perhaps this time it may have been the lobster. However that may be I think that in each case a smile was allowable, and if the smile developed into a roar the victim had no right to be seriously annoyed. After all this match was not a championship, and I have heard of a player laughing at his enemy in a championship. It was that admirable and usually sedate golfer, the late Mr G. F. Smith, who once confessed as much to me. He was playing the third hole at Prestwick, the Cardinal, in the days when the stone wall still existed at the back of the green. His opponent, having a difficult pitch to play, decided – and very wisely – to use the back wall, but his ball pitched on the wrong bump on that rather bumpy green and jumped lightly over the wall. Mr Smith sat down on the green justifiably convulsed with laughter.

In the example from 'Pendennis,' which I quoted at that nightmare dinner party, the Chevalier Strong 'had the grace not to laugh for five minutes, when he exploded into fits of hilarity.' Perhaps that is the kindest as well as the most discreet course. Many things may happen in five minutes, and even the missing of the globe may lose its sting if we hole a long putt immediately afterwards. Of course we who have missed the globe ought to start the laughter ourselves, and we shall be more likely to hole that compensating putt if we do, but there are some heights hard to attain, some walls we cannot putt over.

21

THE MAN WHO HAS DISCOVERED THE SECRET

by Terry Wogan

Many of today's most famous personalities in the world of entertainment list golf as their great pleasure and relaxation. In America, Bob Hope and Frank Sinatra have long been associated with the game, while in Britain, Bruce Forsyth, Jimmy Tarbuck and Terry Wogan are three media stars who play and appear from time to time in charity matches. Terry Wogan, the radio star and television chat show host, may well be the most famous amateur enthusiast of the moment, and certainly he has often talked about his passion for the game and his admiration for the top players.

It is perhaps not surprising that Terry, with his irrepressible Irish sense of humour, should be attuned to the funny side of golf, and in this final selection he splendidly caricatures a few of those infuriating types one can come across in any clubhouse. Though not, as Terry himself earnestly hopes, *too* often . . .

THEN ON THE LONG 16th.....

THE MAN WHO HAS DISCOVERED
THE SECRET

I can hear the discontented muttering even before I start: 'Golf! What in the name of the Sainted Bobby Jones does that oaf know about Golf? He doesn't even pronounce it properly. Any oaf knows its Gowf!' Don't get your ribbed-faced mashie-rublick in a twist. I know that I am a mere 16-handicapped with a new-found tendency to shank, but give us a chance. I've seen Tom Watson take three to get out of a bunker, and Ben Crenshaw miss a tiddler from two feet. I'm sure Jack Nicklaus didn't hit it 300 yards, the first time. Anyway, I don't play often enough. If I did, it would be a different story. I'd be down to single figures in no time. I need new clubs as well, and I could do with a couple of lessons to get rid of that damned shank. I just don't have the time . . .

Who am I kidding? I don't play more often, because if I did, I'd have no excuse. Supposing if I'd played more often, and my handicap went up? No, it's far more comfortable and convenient to the ego to play once a month, and blame the duff shots on lack of practice. 'It usually takes me nine holes to get going, I'm so rusty,' is a favourite ploy of mine. or: 'When you play as little as I do, you lose the feel of the clubs. 'Or, for that matter, yet again: 'These old clubs! Ballesteros couldn't play with 'em! Still, when you play as little as I do, there's no point in buying new ones!'

These bon mots are usually greeted by my playing partners with sympathetic smiles and clicking of the tongue, and telling phrases such as: 'I know – I'd love to get out more often myself.' Or: 'This is great. Do you know, this is the first time I've played since the last game we had, three months ago?' Or, (and this is a killer): 'These aren't even my clubs. I had to borrow the wife's!' This, and all the foregoing, I know to be a downright lie. The man spends every waking moment on the practice ground, and has spent a fortune on clubs and lessons. He eats, drinks and sleeps golf, gets all the magazines, reads all the books and has a putting machine on his bedroom carpet. He has a secret driving net in his back garden, and practises his bunker-shots in the children's sand-pit. Behind their pink gins, down at the Club, they call him 'The Lying Swine'. . .

There are many like him, of course, but he is only one category of bounder, with which the average golf club teems. Of the many examples that spring readily to mind, let me enumerate but a few, gentle remaining readers:

'The Bandit': Close-bosom friend of our chum, the aforesaid 'Lying Swine'. For the Bandit lies, too, only he lies about his handicap. It is the Pariah, the Unclean. People leave the bar in a marked manner upon his entrance or stare pointedly into their halves of bitter. He cares not a jot, or tittle. There are few more brazen than 'The Bandit'. He plays in no club competitions, for this would mean that his handicap (26) would have to be adjusted to his abilities (12). He is content to take money from the unsuspecting, and clocks, decanters, vases, cutlery, and whatever else he can win at Society Outings. And where does this rogue golfer get his handicap? From the Sick and Indigent Roomkeepers' Golfing Society with whom, naturally, he never plays. Otherwise his handicap would have to be adjusted etc. etc. etc. The bandit takes most of his ill-gotten gains from another type, the gullible, 'Man Who Has Discovered The Secret'.

'The Man Who Has Discovered The Secret' has usually been playing the game for about five years. Five hard, unre-warding years of scuffling, shanking, scuffling and swearing. Five years of patronising from other golfers: 'Don't be silly. Everybody has to start . . .' Five years of unconscionable expense – 'My God, the lessons alone run into four figures!'

Then, out of a sky full of rainbows, comes the day. He walks into the Club bar, his face suffused with the light of revelation: 'I've discovered it!' he shouts, to nobody in particular, and everybody in general. 'I've got the secret!' Wiser heads smile knowingly, the Secretary buries his head in his toasted ham and cheese sandwich. 'It's so simple, I don't know how it's taken me so long!' Just a little adjustment to the grip (swing, legs, shoulders, whatever) and everything fell into place! I can't wait to get out there again! He accepts The Bandit's ready challenge, goes out, loses The Secret, the game (9 and 8) and 50 quid . . .

Then there's every club's untouchable: The Bore. The Bore, or to be more precise, The Bores, fall into two clearly defined categories: a) The Bar Bore, and b) The Playing Bore. The Bar Bore is the less dangerous, because you can spot him (and hear him) a mile off. Anybody foolish enough to come within an arm's reach is button-holed with our hero's meticulous recounting of the round he has just played: 'Well, I stood up on the first tee, and took out my one iron. I lined up, then slowly back, keeping my body absolutely still and . . .' So the long night wears on, as he remembers not only that Round, but every Round he has ever played, and every shot he ever played in them. Many a strong man has woken up screaming in the night, after an evening with the Bar Bore. Bad and all as he is though, he cannot hold a candle to The Playing Bore. This ugly creature is the more dangerous because you may not recognise him until it's too late. You can be standing on the first tee, before the awful truth dawns: 'I think I'll take my 3-wood. If I connect with this, I can hit it a mile. No, no, no, you idiot! You're dipping your right shoulder!' This to himself, of course. The Playing Bore is not interested in anybody else's game. Even in a Fourball, he's on his own. He hits his shot ('Oh no! no! Head up! Head up!') and walks briskly after it, whether his partners have played their shots or not. He putts out of turn, ('All wrong! All wrong! The hole won't come to the ball, you idiot!') never tends the flag for his partners' putts, nor helps to look for their lost balls ('Anybody see mine?').

There are as many types in the average golf club as there are lost balls in Turnberry. This has been a brief inadequate glossary, and I'm sure you have favourites of your own, like: The Rule Book ('My hole, I think. I didn't concede you that putt'). The Shall Not Pass ('No you can't play through, we're playing a match'). The Fresh Air Kid ('It was just a practice swing'). The Tiger ('We'll play off the back sticks'). The Rabbit ('Am I holding you up?'). The Gamesman ('Use a wedge. You'll never carry the brook from these'). The Captain ('I'm going to sack the whole bloody Greens Committee').

It's a good job you and I are all right. Fancy a game? You'll have to give me some shots, of course, I don't play very often . . .

ACKNOWLEDGEMENTS

THE EDITOR is grateful to the following authors, agents and publishers for permission to use copyright stories in this collection: The Executors of J. M. Barrie for 'A Braid Hills Mystery'; Punch Publications Ltd for 'The Culbin Game' by C. L. Graves & E. V. Lucas and 'Wartime Golf' by George C. Nash; Mills & Boon Ltd for 'Colonel Belcher's Ghost Story' by Henry Leach; Adam & Charles Black Ltd for 'A One-Ball Match' by Gerald Batchelor; Edward Arnold Ltd for 'Retired Golf' by Harry Graham; Herbert Jenkins Ltd for 'Jan Plays Golf' by A. J. Coles; The Executors of the Estate of A. G. Macdonell for 'Beginner's Luck'; Williams & Norgate Ltd for 'A Caddy's Luck' by Ring Lardner; The Bodley Head for 'A Medieval Hole In One' by Stephen Leacock and 'The Temptation of Admiral Juddy' by Ben Travers; Methuen & Co Ltd for 'An Unlucky Golfer' by A. A. Milne; A. P. Watt Literary Agency for 'Those In Peril On The Tee' by P. G. Wodehouse and 'Is A Golfer A Gentleman?' by A. P. Herbert; A. D. Peters Literary Agency for 'A Heavenly Round' by Paul Gallico; Times Newspapers Ltd for 'Laughter On The Links' by Bernard Darwin; and Terry Wogan for 'The Man Who Has Discovered The Secret'. While every care has been taken to clear permission for use of the